CONTENTS

Fleet in Focus: Yeoward Line
David Burrell   131

A class of three
Clive Guthrie   140

Mersey mishaps   146

Ropner trunk-deck steamers
part 2 *Harold Appleyard*   154

Ferry beyond the Mersey   160

A Liverpool protagonist of sail:
R.W.Leyland and the mighty
DITTON *John Naylon*   162

Long ago in Liverpool   167

Loose ends: Taw Shipyards Ltd.
and Kenneth Shaw   174

The Belfast, Mersey &
Manchester Steamship Co.Ltd.
Roy Fenton   177

Putting the Record straight   188

Sources and
acknowledgements   192

Ships in Focus Publications
Correspondence and editorial:
Roy Fenton
18 Durrington Avenue
London SW20 8NT
0181 879 3527
Orders and photographic:
John & Marion Clarkson
18 Franklands, Longton
Preston PR4 5PD
01772 612855

© 1997 Individual contributors, John Clarkson and Roy Fenton.

All rights reserved. No part of this publication may be reproduced, stored in a retrieval system or transmitted in any form or by any means, electronic, mechanical, photocopying, recording or otherwise, without the written permission of the publisher.

Printed by Amadeus Press Ltd., Huddersfield.
Designed by Hugh Smallwood, John Clarkson and Roy Fenton.
SHIPS IN FOCUS RECORD
ISSN 1363-1675

SHIPS IN
Issue N

Welcome to Issue 3 ... is a special one concentrating on the ships of ... prizes offered for guessing the reasons: both editors gained their taste for ships and shipping around the Mersey, and we also want to help the World Ship Society celebrate its fiftieth birthday in Liverpool during May. Whilst there's a strong Liverpool taste to this issue, we've tried to make it as cosmopolitan as the port itself, and the ships featured will be familiar to many who have never seen the port. We have indulged ourselves with some superb views of Liverpool over one hundred years ago, courtesy of the National Maritime Museum's Picture Department, and a series of photographs of groundings and sinkings in the river. Otherwise we have endeavoured to bring the same wide spread of material as in Issues 1 and 2: even the Mersey tugs and ferries we feature met their fame or their fate well beyond the river.

We would like to thank the many readers who responded to our request to subscribe to *Ships in Focus RECORD:* it is heartening to know so many of you support our aims. Equally, we have been very pleased by the flow of letters which followed previous issues, with comments, corrections and - especially - extra information. Please keep them coming, and we will endeavour to publish as much of this material as we can.

Several readers have requested that extra details are included in the captions to photographs. Whilst sympathetic, we do not want to make these too full of figures, which is why we often include full details of ships in the form of a fleet or yard list - a feature we have unashamedly borrowed from World Ship Society publications! The reader who requested details of type of propulsion makes a good point, and we will endeavour to comply, but where no details of machinery or rig are given it should be assumed that steam reciprocating engines are fitted.

Looking forward to Issue 4, much material has already come in. We can promise features on a post-war cargo liner company, a class of record-breakers built at Swan Hunter, a pleasure steamer operator on the Forth, a further account of a short-lived shipbuilder, a mystery motor tramp that turned up in the Mersey in 1961, plus the concluding part of the story of the DITTON, and several more features. If you've subscribed, sit back and wait: if not, we invite you to reserve your copy of Issue 4 using the form enclosed. If you've enjoyed this issue you clearly like 'real' ships, and you're on our wavelength.

Roy Fenton   John Clarkson

Yeoward Line's ALONDRA: see page 136

AVOCETA

Caledon Shipbuilding & Engineering Co. Ltd., Dundee; 1923, 3,442gt, 319 feet.

Launched on 21st September 1922 AVOCETA entered Yeoward Line Ltd service early in 1923. She was photographed in the Mersey by John McRoberts on 9th April 1932. AVOCETA was in the news in 1936 when she sighted the missing fishing boat GIRL PAT. She was scheduled to cruise to the Baltic in 1939, but the second cruise was cut short at Stockholm in late August and she hurriedly returned to Liverpool, docking on 31st August. Trading to Spain and Portugal she joined convoy HG73 at Gibraltar in September 1941, shortly after the loss of AGUILA. Bound for Britain, this convoy was badly mauled with AVOCETA being sunk by U-203 on 25th September.

Fleet in Focus:
YEOWARD LINE
David Burrell

In 1894 brothers Richard and Lewis Yeoward commenced business in Liverpool as Yeoward Brothers, shipbrokers and fruit merchants. Previous to this Richard had been a shipbroker in London and Lewis a partner in a firm of Liverpool fruit wholesalers. An early interest was established with the Canary Islands, which were visited by Richard during his honeymoon in 1895. Ships were chartered, the first believed to have been in 1898, and an office opened at Las Palmas in 1899.

Business developed and the move from chartering to owning was logical. The first ships purchased came from the Cork Steamship Co. Ltd. With them came a number of distinctive aspects. First nomenclature; the Cork company named its ships after birds, Yeoward followed suit with Spanish bird names commencing with "A—-". Second, the Cork ships were products of W.B. Thompson & Co., Dundee; later the Caledon Shipbuilding & Engineering Co. Ltd. Yeoward remained loyal to the Caledon yard to the end. Third, all the ships purchased were of an unusual three masted, engines three-quarters aft layout. Yeoward developed this style and they were as distinctive at a distance as the fellow Liverpool fleets of Blue Funnel and Bibby. The brothers chose houseflag and funnel markings to reflect their interests, based on the Spanish national colours like those of MacAndrews, Larrinaga and P & O.

The first purchase was AVOCET in August 1900, registered as owned by the first of six single-ship companies. She sailed from Liverpool on her first passage to Lisbon and Las Palmas on 19th October. FULMAR and EGRET followed in 1901 and 1903, renamed ARDEOLA (1) and AVETORO. Also in 1903 a small auxiliary ketch was purchased and renamed ALCA (1) for inter-island service. Sailing from Liverpool on 16th November 1901 ARDEOLA (1) ran down and sank the steamer HERSCHEL (1,693/1884), inbound from Huelva, in the Crosby Channel, and putting back was shortly afterwards in collision with the Westport steamer DAISY.

The limited passenger accommodation on these first ships proved popular, so in 1903 an order for a ship was placed with the Caledon yard. Launched on 17th June 1903 she was named ARDEOLA (2) as the first ship of that name had been sunk in collision with the barque NATUNA (1,137/1885) on 10th December 1903. Of the same dimensions as the ex-Cork ships, ARDEOLA (2) was of slightly greater tonnage as the after well was filled in to give twelve passenger cabins, each with two berths and an optional third settee berth. Three further new ships followed before war broke out in 1914, all progressive developments; AGUILA (1) in 1909, ANDORINHA in 1911 and another ARDEOLA (3), the first to exceed 3,000gt, in 1912. They had 32, 34 and 39 cabins respectively, with the last two also providing four cabins de-luxe (as did all subsequent ships). Another ship was ordered in 1914, but delayed for several years due to the war. ARDEOLA (2) was outclassed, so in 1912 she had been sold to Canadian owners, renamed MORWENNA, and lasted until sunk by U-41 south of Fastnet on 26th May 1915.

With these ships Yeoward developed increasingly popular cruises from Liverpool to Portugal, the Canaries and Madeira which, in the inter-war years, saw the slogan "Sunward by Yeoward" coined and the featuring of actress Jean Harlow on posters.

The outbreak of war in August 1914 found five ships, two elderly ex-Cork cargo ships and the latest three, engaged in trade to Portugal, the Canaries and Madeira. Of these only ANDORINHA and ARDEOLA (3) survived, along with a new AGUILA (2). AGUILA (1) was the first loss on 27th March 1915, U-28 proving the faster when Captain Bannerman tried to outrun the attacker. The press reported "another victim of the German pirates", eight lives were lost and in 1921 the Committee of Lloyd's posthumously awarded Captain Bannerman Lloyd's Silver Medal for Meritorious Services. DON HUGO was purchased and renamed ALONDRA (1) to replace her, but only lasted to 29th December 1916 when she was wrecked on the Irish coast. Captain Bannerman took command of AVETORO and sailed from Barry with coal for Las Palmas on 11th November 1915. AVETORO's end has never been explained and she was posted missing at Lloyd's on 26th January 1916. Later in 1916, on 10th April, Lewis Yeoward died of fever, leaving his older brother alone to control the business.

The last loss was AVOCET. Attacked for the third time by a submarine her luck ran out and unlike the previous occasions she was unable to escape. Shelled by U-50, her Nordenfeldt six-pounder was of little use, the official report stated "Again an ineffective gun had led to the loss of a good ship". Other failed attacks on the ships included a torpedo miss on ARDEOLA (3) and a hit, which failed to explode, on ANDORINHA in October 1917.

The order placed in 1914 proceeded slowly as wartime priorities permitted. Launched in September 1916 as AGUILA (2) she was completed in late 1917. Also in 1917 two Norwegian ships chartered by the Shipping Controller were placed under Yeoward management until returned to their owners in 1919, DRAMMENSEREN (3,188/1894) and MIRJAM (3,374/1904).

ALONDRA (2) loads bananas by man-powered lighters off Santa Cruz, Canary Islands in 1936. *[National Maritime Museum N32719]*

Early in 1920 the six shipowning companies were amalgamated into the Yeoward Line Ltd. As with the earlier companies, the bulk of the shares were in the hands of the Yeoward family, with nominal holdings registered to senior managers. Later that year orders were placed with Caledon for two near sisters of AGUILA (2), delivered as ALONDRA (2) and AVOCETA in 1922 and 1923. Finally, 1927 saw the delivery of the last ship to join the fleet, ALCA (2). The oldest member of the fleet, ANDORINHA of 1911, was sold to the Pacific Steam Navigation Co. in 1929 and renamed CHAMPERICO. The same year Richard Yeoward retired, leaving control with his son Raymond, who had been admitted a partner of Yeoward Brothers in 1924.

Yeoward's trade suffered from the onset of the Depression in 1929, also the outbreak of the Spanish Civil War in 1936. ALONDRA (2) was sold in 1938 and joined ANDORINHA on the Chilean coast. In July 1938 Raymond Yeoward stated the intention to renew the fleet, but this was not to be as six months later a joint MacAndrews-Yeoward Service was inaugurated with MacAndrews modern P-class motorships.

The outbreak of war found AGUILA (2) sailing from Tenerife for home, ALCA (2) in Liverpool and ARDEOLA (3) loading in the Bristol Channel. AVOCETA was cruising in the Baltic. ALCA (2) and AGUILA (2) both had inconclusive brushes with submarines in 1940 and later that year ALCA (2) was commissioned as a controlled minelayer base ship.

1941 was catastrophic for the Yeoward fleet. Within six weeks AGUILA (2) and AVOCETA wre lost with only 49 survivors from the 331 passengers and crew. ARDEOLA (3) survived until late 1942 when, trying to slip through enemy waters with supplies for Malta, she was captured. During and after the war four ships were managed for the Ministry of War Transport, the Danish SLESVIG (3,098/1938) from 1943-4 and three prizes from 1945-6, EMPIRE KENNETT (2,319/1926), EMPIRE LEA (2,563/1942) and EMPIRE WEY (2,645/1944).

Only ALCA (2) remained when peace was restored, and she needed extensive dockyard work, having undergone major alterations for war service, but was able to take her first postwar sailing from Liverpool in May 1946. Additional tonnage came from an agreement with Christian Clausen, Copenhagen, who became a director of Yeoward Line from 1952 to 1955. This saw DORRIT CLAUSEN (1,396/1947), BJORN CLAUSEN (1,450/1949) and VERNA CLAUSEN (2,081/1948) employed. When ALCA (2) was broken up in 1955 Captain Frith was offered a command by Clausen, taking his DUCHY OF NORMANDY (ex VERNA CLAUSEN) under the British flag until retiring in 1959.

Clausen resigned as a director in December 1955 and endeavoured to operate his own service, without success. Yeoward turned to Manchester Liners and MANCHESTER VANGUARD (1,662/1956) and MANCHESTER VENTURE (1,662/1956) were employed for three years in the fruit season. Built for service into the Great Lakes, the Yeoward Line work fitted into the closed season when the Lakes were icebound.

A year of change, 1959, saw the third generation of the family, Anthony Yeoward, take the helm. Yeoward Brothers was converted into a limited company and Yeoward Line was wound up. The contract to ship Canary produce was lost to Naviera Aznar, with Yeoward Brothers as Liverpool agents. For the next twenty years the cruise business was rebuilt with ships like MONTE UMBE (9,971/1959), before Aznar's financial difficulties led to collapse in 1979. Since then the Nissui Line has shipped Canary produce for exporters with Yeoward handling the ships in the U.K.

Today Yeoward Brothers Ltd are still shipbrokers, but their other original trade, fruit merchants, is history. Diversification has led them to become a small group with several lines of business as they move through the early years of their second century with the fourth generation of the family taking their place in the management team.

AVETORO
W.B. Thompson & Co. Ltd., Dundee; 1890, 1,255gt, 256 feet

Built as EGRET for the Cork Steamship Co. Ltd., Cork, she passed to the Avetoro Steam Ship Co. Ltd. in July 1903, managed by Yeoward Brothers, Liverpool. Renamed AVETORO she was chartered to R. Bewley for nearly two years in 1913-1915, under the Russian flag. Only months after returning she sailed from Barry on 11th November 1915 on charter to Sivewright, Bacon & Co., Manchester, with coal for Las Palmas. Sighted soon afterwards by the Allen liner SCOTIAN, she was never seen again and was posted missing at Lloyd's on 26th January 1916. *[F.W. Hawks]*

ANDORINHA
Caledon Shipbuilding & Engineering Co. Ltd., Dundee; 1911, 2,548gt, 290 feet.

Completed for the newly formed Andorinha Steam Ship Co. Ltd, managed by Yeoward Bros, Liverpool, ANDORINHA was the third ship purpose-built for the line and had a passenger certificate for 115 people. Transferred to the new Yeoward Line Ltd in 1920, she was sold in 1929 and spent the next few years as the CHAMPERICO of the Pacific Steam Navigation Co. on the West Coast of South America. They sold her in 1934 to Chilean owners and as VINA DEL MAR she spent the rest of her career under that flag, much of it in the service of Empresa Maritima del Estado. Reduced to a storeship in 1960 some years later she grounded and today lies abandoned on the shore at Puerto Chacabuco, as in the photograph to the right. *[Middle: World Ship Photo Library; right David Burrell collection]*

ARDEOLA (3)
Caledon Shipbuilding & Engineering Co. Ltd., Dundee; 1912, 3,140gt, 310 feet.
Launched on 17th July 1912, ARDEOLA was the last ship delivered before the First World War, which she survived. Originally owned by the Ardeola Steam Ship Co. Ltd she passed to Yeoward Line Ltd. in 1920. Heightened Middle East tension when Italy invaded Abyssinia in 1935 saw her requisitioned as a base ship at Aden. Returned to Yeowards in 1936 her passenger certificate was not renewed. War service saw her chosen in 1942, with TADORNA, for Operation Cropper, an attempt to run supplies to Malta. Both ships were captured by Vichy forces off Tunisia and, as a prize, ARDEOLA became the Italian ADERNO, only to be sighted and sunk by HMS TORBAY on 23rd July 1943. On the right, ARDEOLA is in dock with AGUILA during September 1932.
[Middle: David Burrell collection]

VALDES
Craig, Taylor & Co. Ltd., Stockton-on-Tees; 1914, 2,233gt, 265 feet
MacAndrews' VALDES was a second wartime purchase in March 1916. Although owned by the Avetoro Steam Ship Co. Ltd., intended renaming as AVETORO was never implemented. Under requisition as a transport for British forces on the Western Front, she was sunk south of Portland Bill by U-84 on 17th February 1917 whilst on a voyage from Manchester to Cherbourg with flour and hay. *[David Burrell collection]*

AGUILA (2)
Caledon Shipbuilding & Engineering Co. Ltd., Dundee; 1917, 3,255gt, 315 feet.

Although ordered in 1914 wartime exigencies saw her launch delayed until 12th September 1916. A further year was to elapse before she was completed in November 1917. At Tenerife when war was declared in 1939 she had a brush with a submarine in August 1940. The following year she sailed from Liverpool in convoy OG71 for Gibraltar. The Commodore was on board and the full passenger list included the first party of young Wrens to be posted abroad. Attacked, the convoy suffered heavy losses including AGUILA, torpedoed by U-201 on 19th August. Few survived, none of them Wrens. Sixteen were picked up, some to be lost soon after on EMPIRE OAK, and only nine were landed at Gibraltar.

ALONDRA (2)
Caledon Shibuilding & Engineering Co. Ltd., Dundee; 1922, 3,445gt, 319 feet.

The first postwar addition to the fleet, ALONDRA was launched on 30th November 1921, a year after the contract was signed and joined the fleet of the recently formed Yeoward Line Ltd. The current owners of VINA DEL MAR (ex ANDORINHA), the Chilean State Railways, purchased her in 1938 and she sailed from Liverpool for Valparaiso on 21st October. For the next two decades they ran together until ALONDRA was sold in 1959 and broken up the following year.

The upper photograph shows ALONDRA in the Mersey; in the lower shot she is anchored off Ponta Delgada in 1936. *[Bottom: National Maritime Museum N32717]*

ALCA (2)
Caledon Shipbuilding & Engineering Co. Ltd., Dundee; 1927, 3,712gt, 319 feet.

The last ship to join the Yeoward Line Ltd, in August 1927, ALCA was to be Yeoward's sole survivor of the Second World War. Commissioned in 1940 as a controlled minelayer base ship she maintained controlled minefields off ports and anchorages. Based at Freetown until 1942, she then returned to home waters to work at Scapa Flow and elsewhere. Extensively altered for this service, she was rebuilt and returned to Yeowards in 1946 as in the lower photograph taken in October 1949. Her last Canary Islands voyage ended in May 1954 and, after a charter between Denmark and Greenland, she went for scrap at Preston in 1955.

MANAGED AND CHARTERED SHIPS

SLESVIG as KRONOBORG
Helsingors Jernskibs og Maskinbyggeri A/S, Elsinore; 1938, 3,098gt, 351 feet.
Pictured as the Finnish flag KRONOBORG, SLESVIG was completed in late 1938 for Copenhagen owners. Laid up at Las Palmas when Denmark was occupied she came under Ministry of War Transport control in 1943 and until 1944 was managed by Yeoward Bros., Liverpool. Management then went to Furness, Withy & Co Ltd until returned to her owners in 1946. Sold and renamed in 1957 another sale in 1969 saw her named TIURI before being broken up at Shanghai in 1972.

BJORN CLAUSEN
Aalborg Vaerft A/S, Aalborg; 1949, 1,450gt, 296 feet.
Following the sale of their own ships, Yeowards maintained their service with chartered tonnage, some of which painted up their funnel colours. Owned by the C. Clausen Dampskibsred A/S (Christian Clausen, manager), Copenhagen, BJORN CLAUSEN was sold to French owners in 1961 and became LES ANNASSERS. A further sale saw her renamed HOPE under the Greek flag until she caught fire and became a constructive total loss at Piraeus on 12th October 1974. *[World Ship Photo Library].*

MONTE URQUIOLA (above)
Sociedad Espanola de Construccion Naval S.A., Bilbao; 1949, 7,723gt, 487 feet.
Commenced in 1943 and launched as MONASTERIO DE GUADALUPE in 1946, but only completed, as MONTE URQUIOLA, in late 1949. Sold by Naviera Aznar S.A to Maldivian owners in 1974 she was renamed CLIMAX GARNET until broken up in 1978. *[George Scott collection]*

MANCHESTER VANGUARD (below)
A.G. Weser Werk Seebeck, Bremerhaven; 1956, 1,662gt, 258 feet.
Built for Manchester Liners trade into the Great Lakes before the St. Lawrence Seaway was opened, MANCHESTER VANGUARD became redundant when larger ships could penetrate into the Mid-West and was sold to the General Steam Navigation Co. Ltd. in 1963 to become SHELDRAKE alongside the former MANCHESTER VENTURE. Later names carried included BAT GOLAN (1968), WOODCHUCK (1974), SELATAN MAJU (1975) and WIHAR I (1981) before being broken up in 1985. *[F.W. Hawks]*

MONTE DE LA ESPERANZA (above)
Pusey & Jones Cpn, Wilmington; 1938, 3,258gt, 298 feet.
Completed as CAVALIER for the Philadelphia & Norfolk Steamboat Co. Inc., Philadelphia, she carried the names MONADNOCK (1942), CAVALIER (1947) and KARUKARA (1949), before passing to Naviera Aznar S.A., Bilbao, as MONTE DE LA ESPERANZA in 1952. They retained her until she went for breaking up in 1965. *[F.W. Hawks]*

MONTE ARUCAS (below)
Compañia Euskalduna de Construccion y Reparacion de Buques, Bilbao; 1956, 4,691gt, 388 feet.
Sold by Naviera Aznar S.A. in 1976 to Greek owners she became the Panamanian flag NISSOS KERKYRA. In 1980 she returned to Spanish ownership, but under the Panamanian flag, as the ATLANTIC FREEZER. Shortly before being lost she became BARDINI REEFER, owned in Las Palmas. On 16th December 1982 she took fire near Castletown Bere and sank two days later. *[George Scott collection]*

A CLASS OF THREE
Clive Guthrie

This is the strange story of three small motor tugs which were all built by the same shipyard, to the same design and ordered by the same owner. Completed by W.J.Yarwood & Sons Ltd., Northwich, Cheshire as lighterage tugs for J. Rea Ltd. of Liverpool, they were the 'tree' prefixed 'garth' tugs, the ELMGARTH, PINEGARTH and CHERRYGARTH. Their later owners used them for ship towage, doing a job for which essentially they were not designed, a change which was to have dire consequences. This is an account of the fateful coincidence which befell these tugs. But first, we will trace the background to their building.

In 1902 the business of Rea Transport Co. Ltd. was founded to operate a harbour coaling and lighterage service based at Liverpool, to attend the bunkering of ships and provide water transport between docks, warehouses, and factories on the Mersey and the Manchester Ship Canal. This company was a subsidiary of R. & J.H.Rea Ltd. which in turn was a partnership formed in 1879 by two brothers, Russell and James H. Rea. The majority of the Rea Transport fleet of tugs and barges were new construction by the Lytham Shipbuilding & Engineering Co. Ltd., Lytham, Lancashire. By 1912 the tug fleet consisted of FELLGARTH (66/02), EDENGARTH (66/03), STANEGARTH (45/10) and ULLSGARTH (45/12), all steam powered. By April 1919 these tugs were owned by Rea Ltd. and remained in Rea's ownership for the next half century with the exception of the STANEGARTH. This tug was sold to the Sharpness New Docks & Gloucester & Birmingham Navigation Co. in 1933.

In 1958 Rea Ltd. took delivery of the motor tug INCEGARTH (34/58), built by Isaac Pimblott of Northwich, Cheshire, which replaced the ULLSGARTH (broken up in 1958). The next steam tugs to leave the lighterage fleet were the FELLGARTH and EDENGARTH, both being sold for scrap and replaced by the motor tugs ELMGARTH and PINEGARTH. The last of the trio to be built was the CHERRYGARTH, which replaced the steam tug REDCROFT (56/36), also having been built by Yarwoods. This steam tug had joined the fleet in October 1960 when Reas acquired the lighterage business of William Bate & Co. Ltd. of Liverpool. The REDCROFT was sold for breaking up in March 1964. It should be mentioned that, since 1946, the FELLGARTH, EDENGARTH and

The steam tug FELLGARTH was completed by the Lytham Shipbuilding & Engineering Co. Ltd. in July 1902, and survived until December 1959 when she was delivered to William Cubbin (Birkenhead) Ltd. for breaking up. Here she is seen soon after the First World War with an open wheelhouse. The crew members repay close study: could they by any chance be female?

The motor tug INCEGARTH (above right, taken September 1962) was sold in 1970 and carried the name DOROTHY FERRAN for some years. As INCEGARTH once again, she was sold for breaking up in 1994. REDCROFT (below right) is seen in the colours of original owners William Bates.

Both EDENGARTH (above left, taken 1956) and ULLSGARTH (below left, taken 5th August 1953) were built at Lytham in 1903 and 1912, respectively. Both were broken up by William Cubbin (Birkenhead) Ltd. Attention is again directed to the crew: what precisely is the man up the ladder doing on EDENGARTH?

141

ELMGARTH in September 1965.

ULLSGARTH were registered as owned by the Rapid Coaling Syndicate Ltd., another Rea subsidiary formed in 1912 which was managed in the late 1950s by Frederick J. Durrant, also manager of Rea Ltd., being succeeded in the 1960s by William M.S.H. Fleming.

During their last full year (1971) in Rea's ownership, the ELMGARTH, PINEGARTH and CHERRYGARTH were, between them, engaged in moving the last regular commercial traffic to use the Upper Mersey Navigation. On spring tides one tug and two barges loaded with drums of carbide made their way up the twisting channel of the Mersey, having taken the pilot at Dingle Oil Jetty, to the Weston Mersey Lock entrance to the Manchester Ship Canal. The carbide, en route from Port Talbot, had been transhipped into barges at Liverpool. At the M.S.C. lock, the tug exchanged the loaded barges with unladen ones, and returned down river. The carbide was delivered by M.S.C. tugs to the I.C.I. chemical works at Weston Point, near Runcorn. The Upper Mersey Navigation closed to shipping in early 1973.

By the end of the 1960s the lighterage business was feeling the effects of road transport and the advent of containerisation - the latter was of course to have a great effect on other maritime activities. In this climate, Rea Ltd. decided to withdraw from lighterage, a business which they had successfully built up over the previous seventy years and, with that withdrawal, came the disposal of ELMGARTH, PINEGARTH and CHERRYGARTH. As these were modern tugs, being only ten years old, had Reas wisely decided that they were unsuitable for ship handling?

In late 1972, ELMGARTH sailed from the Mersey for the North Sea, having been sold to Lowestoft owners. By early 1973 she had passed to Pevensey Castle Ltd., also of Lowestoft, with the new name of BARKIS. She was now to be used by her new owners only for ship handling.

On the 16th August 1976, at 08.40 hours, the BARKIS was manoeuvring to give assistance to the Cypriot motor ship JUPITER (voyage Hull to Alexandria) into Lowestoft, when a collision occurred between these two vessels, which caused the BARKIS to roll over and sink about half mile north of Lowestoft harbour and 100 metres off the shore. Sadly the sinking resulted in the loss of one of the crew of four on board BARKIS, the other three being rescued by the Lowestoft pilot launch. Although attempts were made to salvage the tug, these were unsuccessful and the BARKIS was declared a total loss.

PINEGARTH was sold by Reas in 1972 to a Swansea owner, who renamed her SEAN CLAIRE. By February 1974 she had also passed to a Lowestoft company, the Colne Fishing Co. Ltd., who renamed her ALA. Here she would surely have rubbed shoulders (or should it be fenders) with her sister tug BARKIS.

During the early hours of 26th January 1986 the British registered motor tanker LYNDEB, owned by M.W. Beer & Co., Gibraltar, was on a voyage from

PINEGARTH in September 1965.

Dunkirk to Hull when she ran aground about 600 yards north of Lowestoft. The motor tug ALA was summoned to assist and during the attempt to refloat the LYNDEB, ALA capsized and sank at 01.55 hours. Fortunately, ALA's crew of three were rescued by the motor standby safety vessel JAMAICA (402/58). The LYNDEB was refloated by the motor tug ANGLIAN (98/64) at 03.15 hours and continued her voyage to Hull. As with BARKIS, attempts were made to retrieve ALA, but they were unsuccessful and Trinity House took charge of the wreck with effect from 7th February 1986 for the purpose of disposal by demolition. A curious fact about the loss of ALA, was that she was purchased by Colne Fishing Co. Ltd. to replace their motor tug MARDYKE (37/57) which herself had overturned and sunk on 21st December 1973. This loss occurred when the MARDYKE was attempting to refloat the motor trawler GRENADA (205/55) which had gone aground on the Corton Bank off Lowestoft. The GRENADA was owned by the Dragon Fishing Co. Ltd., Lowestoft, but managed by the Colne Fishing Co. Ltd, owners of the lost tug BARKIS.

The third and final tug of the trio built by Yarwoods for Rea Ltd. was the CHERRYGARTH. Although not completed until 1963 and having spent only nine years in their ownership she was put up for disposal. With Reas withdrawal from lighterage she was sold to Bulk Cargo Handling Services Ltd., Liverpool (a subsidiary of Alexandra Towing Co. Ltd.) in October 1972. With B.C.H.S. Ltd. CHERRY, as she was renamed, continued working as a lighterage tug, often towing barges up the Manchester Ship Canal, mainly delivering maize to Brown & Polson Ltd., the cornflour manufacturers, at Trafford Park. CHERRY continued her service on the Mersey until 1978 when she was transferred to the Southampton towing fleet of her parent company, Alexandra Towing. It was here that fate played its part.

The Norwegian motor vessel TANAFJORD owned by Den Norske Amerikalinje A/S, Oslo, was inward bound to Southampton from Mauritius during the early morning of the 18th December 1978, sailing later that day for Caen. The tug CHERRY was assisting the TANAFJORD to Berth 202 when she overturned and sank, fortunately with no loss of life. On 20th December, Risdon Beazley Marine Ltd. of Southampton were given the task of recovering CHERRY using the salvage vessel SEAFORD (791/73). By 27th December, CHERRY had been righted and delivered to Husband's Shipyard Ltd. Cracknore Hard, Marchwood, for a decision on her future. Lady luck obviously smiled on her.

CHERRY was purchased by Metal Recoveries Ltd. of Newhaven in December 1978 and after renovation was sold in 1980 to Piraeus owners and renamed NISSOS KALAMOS. After several changes of owner and renaming MADONNA, by 1995 she was no longer listed on the Greek Shipping Register and it must be assumed that she was broken up.

The fact that these three tugs all suffered the same fate of capsizing and sinking must surely be a unique occurrence to befall a class of three identical vessels. The result is all the more bizarre considering that the tugs were performing a task for which they were not basically designed.

ELMGARTH
O.N. 301358 62 gt. 68.0 x 18.6 x 8.6 feet
Oil engine 6-cyl. by Ruston & Hornsby Ltd., Lincoln; 400 BHP.
15.6.1960: Launched by W.J. Yarwood & Sons Ltd., Northwich (Yard No. 927) for Rea Ltd. (Frederick J. Durrant, manager), Liverpool as ELMGARTH.
14.9.1960: Completed.
1972: Sold to the Lowestoft Fishing Vessel Owners Association, Lowestoft.
1972: Sold to Pevensey Castle Ltd. (Maurice Horabin, manager), Lowestoft and renamed BARKIS.
16.8.1976: Capsized and sank half a mile north of Lowestoft harbour in position 52.28.36N by 01.46.32E whilst towing the Cypriot motor vessel JUPITER (1,594/64, ex-CLAREBROOK).

PINEGARTH
O.N. 301370 63 gt 68.0 x 18.6 x 8.6 feet
Oil engine 6-cyl. by Ruston & Hornsby Ltd., Lincoln; 400 BHP.
7.12.1960: Launched by W.J. Yarwood & Sons Ltd., Northwich (Yard No. 928) for Rea Ltd. (Frederick J. Durrant, manager), Liverpool as PINEGARTH.
3.1961: Completed.
1973: Sold to Gerald Williams, Swansea and renamed SEAN CLAIRE.
2.1974: Sold to Colne Fishing Co. Ltd. (John H. Legget, manager), Lowestoft and renamed ALA.
26.1.1986: Capsized and sank 600 yards north of Lowestoft in position 52.28.18N by 01.45.97E whilst assisting the motor tanker LYNDEB (453/51).

CHERRYGARTH
O.N. 303898 64 gt 68.0 x 18.6 x 8.6 feet
Oil engine 6-cyl. by Ruston & Hornsby Ltd., Lincoln; 400 BHP.
30.8.1963: Launched by W.J. Yarwood & Sons Ltd., Northwich (Yard No. 941) for Rea Ltd. (Frederick J. Durrant, manager), Liverpool as CHERRYGARTH.
10.1972: Sold to Bulk Cargo Handling Services Ltd., Liverpool and renamed CHERRY.
1978: Owners became Alexandra Towing Co.Ltd., Liverpool, and transferred to Southampton.
18.12.1978: Capsized and sank whilst assisting the Norwegian motor vessel TANAFJORD (7,365/76) at Southampton.
27.12.78: Raised.
22.12.1979: Sold to Metal Recoveries Ltd., Newhaven.
26.8.1980: Sold to Georgios Portolos, United Tugboats Ltd. (Portolos Salvage S.A., managers), Piraeus, Greece and renamed NISSOS KALAMOS.
1990: Sold to D. Melissanidis, Mikrasiatiki Naftiki Eteria (Aegean Petroleum International Trading Ltd., managers) and renamed MADONNA.
1994: Principal owner of Aegean Petroleum International Trading Ltd. became John Karras.
1995: No longer listed in Greek Shipping Register and presumed broken up.

CHERRYGARTH.

ALA, ex-PINEGARTH, at Great Yarmouth in 1976.

BARKIS, ex-ELMGARTH, at Great Yarmouth in 1976.

CHERRY, ex-CHERRYGARTH, heads upriver with lighters (below). The lighter to port is the D.W. WILLIAMS, built at Northwich in 1920 as a steam derrick barge for Anchor-Brocklebank Line. By coincidence the other lighter, NEW CONVEYOR, and the tug were also built by Yarwoods at Northwich.

MERSEY MISHAPS

THE WRECKED "ARMAGH"

KING ORRY (opposite page, top)
Cammell Laird & Co. Ltd., Birkenhead; 1913, 1,877gt, 300 feet
The least dangerous, but possibly the most embarassing, mishap of those recorded here involved the third KING ORRY of the Isle of Man Steam Packet Co. Ltd. At the height of the 1921 season, on 19th August, the turbine steamer went aground in dense fog at 1.30 pm 100 feet east of the Rock Lighthouse, which can be seen in the photograph. No fewer than 1,300 passengers were on board, rescue being a simple matter of waiting for the tide to ebb and putting ladders alongside. KING ORRY was refloated with the help of tugs on the morning tide of 20th August, very little the worse for the adventure.

This was a very small incident in what began and ended as an adventurous career. The nearly-new steamer had been taken up early during the First World War, served as a boarding steamer, a target tug, and latterly was disguised as a neutral. War service culminated with leading the German High Seas Fleet into Scapa Flow to surrender. KING ORRY was in the thick of things again during the Second World War, but luck ran out at Dunkirk where she was bombed and sunk on 30th May 1940.

DURHAM COAST (opposite page, bottom)
Goole Shipbuilding & Repairing Co. Ltd., Goole; 1912, 783gt, 215 feet
It is clear from the gash in her port bow that DURHAM COAST had had a close encounter with another ship, but it was some time after the incident before the other combatant was identified. When the United States tanker SUNOIL (7,157/16), inward bound from Philadelphia, docked at Manchester it became apparent that it was her that had collided with the outward-bound Coast Lines' vessel off New Brighton. The incident took place at about 2.00 am on 7th June 1924, and also involved the schooner NELLIE FLEMING (119/84).

Some of DURHAM COAST's cargo was discharged on the beach, although part floated out by itself. She was patched and refloated on 11th June and taken to Vittoria Dock, Birkenhead to complete unloading. DURHAM COAST went on to enjoy a long career: sold to owners in Calcutta in 1946 she was not broken up until 1957.

ARMAGH (this page, top)
Swan Hunter and Wigham Richardson Ltd., Wallsend-on-Tyne; 1917, 12,269g 531 feet
On 15th December 1923 the ARMAGH grounded on Taylor's Bank Revetment in the Crosby Channel and broke her back, beginning what turned out to be an epic operation to salvage her valuable general cargo. Each day the Liverpool and Glasgow Salvage Association's representative filed a breezy report of operations which was duly published in Lloyd's Lists, revealing many intimate details of the salvage work.

With ARMAGH's engine room flooded, there was no steam available for the winches, and the first task was for the salvage steamer RANGER to put a portable boiler aboard so that cargo could be worked. Described as 'fine Manchester goods', the cargo comprised a cross-section of the incredible variety of manufactured items which were exported to the British Empire: from Crossley motor cars to chemicals, and from tramway poles to tinplate. Monks' coaster KATHERINE was engaged to take off the salvaged cargo, about one hundred tons of which were taken out each working day.

Although salvage work was attempted from dawn to dusk six days a week, operations could not be conducted every day. Adverse weather often meant that 'boating' was impossible, and there were also human factors to delay progress. On 29th March 1924 the steam lighter PRIDE O'TH 'WEAVER stranded on the revetment, later getting off but preventing work that day. A Liverpool dock strike also delayed unloading of the salvaged cargo from KATHERINE.

Cargo from the ARMAGH became progressively more difficult to work. The hull was disappearing into the sand, a process which was particularly rapid during spring tides whose scouring action meant it could sink as much as a foot each day. By April, cargo could only be got out by divers. During May a day was spent breaking out a steam wagon which was obstructing work in No. 2 hold, an operation complicated by the need to rig special tackle to lift such a heavy load.

The Salvage Association's work was restricted to holds number 1 to 4. As the photo makes clear, the after holds were submerged. Here the Kymo Shipping Co. Ltd., basically a steam lighterage operation, attempted some salvage work during January but achieved little or nothing, and there are no reports of their doing further work.

By 22nd July 1924 the Liverpool and Glasgow Salvage Association had concluded that work on ARMAGH was no longer worthwhile, the remaining cargo in the forward holds now being buried in silt. They abandoned operations, and left it to the Mersey Docks and Harbour Board to cut down the wreck.

At the time of her wreck the ARMAGH had just set off on a voyage from Liverpool to Brisbane, and although she was sailing for Federal Line her owners were the Union Steam Ship Co. of New Zealand Ltd.

OKLAHOMA (above)
John Readhead and Sons Ltd., South Shields; 1917, 4,579gt, 400 feet
OKLAHOMA was one of Liverpool's worst peacetime fires, putting several other ships in danger and being destroyed herself. The French steamer arrived at Sandon Dock from Talcahuano, Chile on 13th October 1929 and two days later fire broke out in her cargo which included nitrate, cotton and sugar. Several explosions occurred due to gases given off by the nitrate and pieces of metal, bags of sugar and burning timber were hurled over adjacent sheds, causing damage and starting small fires on other ships in the dock.

The fire was concentrated in the fore part of OKLAHOMA, which sank and some of the holds collapsed. As salvage operations began it was necessary to sink the afterpart. Nevertheless, some cargo was discharged, and the French steamer ST. JOSEPH (5,796/12) called on her way home from Talcahuano to collect it.

Damage to the OKLAHOMA's hull was such that conventional methods of raising her failed, and the Mersey Docks and Harbour Board resorted to draining Sandon Dock so that she could be patched up. The photograph shows the scene sometime after November 18th when the dock had been run dry. OKLAHOMA was refloated on 1st February 1930 and immediately towed across the river and beached at Tranmere, where J. Hornby and Co. broke her up.

The ship had been built for the Dalgleish Steam Ship Co. Ltd., Newcastle as WARKWORTH. In 1923 she was sold to a London company and named OKLAHOMA, a name she kept when purchased by Compagnie Genérale Transatlantique in 1926.

ARCHITECT
Charles Connell and Co. Ltd., Glasgow; 1912, 5,421gt, 411 feet
T. & J. Harrison's ARCHITECT (above) was a case of an apparently rather trivial grounding leading to the total loss of a vessel and most of her valuable cargo. She left Brunswick Dock about 8.00am on 29th October 1933 outward bound for Tampico with a cargo consisting of machinery and other manufactured goods. A few minutes later she was aground on the north bank of the Mersey near the Dock entrance. She was refloated on the evening tide, but was making water so fast that that she had to be put ashore again off the old Coburg Dock entrance.

Strenuous efforts were begun the next morning to remove her cargo, with hundreds of men and many barges being used. But she was lying with her bow on one sandbank and her stern on another, and that night she broke her back. Despite her being well inside the river, ARCHITECT's position rapidly deteriorated in the prevailing north westerlies and she began to break up. She was also sinking into the sandbank, so that by 3rd November her main deck was awash at high water. The top photograph opposite, dated 7th November 1933, shows her in this condition, whilst a week later (second photo) the funnel had collapsed. Her topmasts and derricks went next (third photo) but the steam lighter alongside suggests that attempts were still being made to remove cargo.

As the bottom photograph opposite shows, just a bare hull remained by 14th April 1934, and accessible parts of this were being removed by the Mersey Docks and Harbour Board.

[Second from top: Fred Parkinson collection]

EMPRESS OF CANADA (above)
John Brown and Co. Ltd., Clydebank 1928, 20,022gt, 582 feet
This aerial view shows the aftermath of one of the biggest post-war salvage operations in Liverpool Docks, that involving the EMPRESS OF CANADA. On 25th January 1953 fire broke out whilst she was lying in Gladstone Dock, and she subsequently capsized. Several photographs have been published of the righting operations, which were successfully concluded on 6th March, but this view of her being towed into the river is much less familiar. It was probably taken on 1st September when, after dry docking, the burnt-out hulk was being handed over to the Dutch tug ZWARTE ZEE for towing to breakers at Spezia.
[National Maritime Museum P2955]

MATRONA (opposite, bottom)
Barclay, Curle and Co. Ltd., Glasgow; 1918, 7,938gt, 450 feet
As the photographs here testify, when a ship reaches sheltered waters - or even a dock - it is still not safe from danger. Perhaps the most hazardous period in port is during modifications, as those working on the MATRONA discovered on 30th October 1947. As Elder, Dempster's ABA the twin-screw motorship had seen extensive service as a hospital ship during the Second World War, but soon after being handed back to her owners she was sold to the Bawtry Steamship Co. Ltd., behind which was the Greek Livanos family. MATRONA was slowly being refitted for these owners in Bidston Dock, Birkenhead, when she suddenly rolled over. Those on board must have had some warning, as they escaped along a plank to the tanker FICUS lying alongside. It took until 8th June 1948 to right MATRONA, and this was only achieved after much of her upperworks had been cut away. After mud was pumped out she was refloated on 13th July 1948, and almost immediately drydocked, but the hulk had no future and arrived at Barrow-in-Furness on 4th October to be broken up.

LURCHER (this page, top)
Scott and Sons, Bowling; 1939, 859gt, 211 feet
Giving a ship the name LURCHER seems to be inviting trouble. Coast Lines Ltd. bestowed this name on the SAXON QUEEN in 1959 when transferred from subsidiary Queenship Navigation Ltd. to the parent company. She was to participate in the Link Line unit load service on the Irish Sea, her running mates also carrying names of dog breeds. Just after dark on 21st January 1961, LURCHER was leaving Liverpool for Glasgow when run down by the Greek motor vessel STAMATIOS G. EMBIRICOS (8,878/56), which was leaving for Hampton Roads. LURCHER sank within ten minutes off New Brighton, her crew of 12 being rescued by the prompt action of Rea's tug BANGARTH.

The motor coaster lay in 60 feet of water, and was raised by the classic method of putting wires beneath her and lifting her with camels. On March 30th she was refloated and taken to Morpeth Dock, Birkenhead, but required pumping out every five hours. LURCHER was briefly dry-docked in May to patch her up to avoid the necessity of pumping - the crude patch can be seen in this photograph - but was considered worthless and was abandoned to the Mersey Docks and Harbour Board in November. However, it was not until 31st March 1964 that she arrived at Preston to be broken up by T.W. Ward Ltd. *[Roy Fenton collection]*

SERTAN (this page, bottom)
Scheepswerf 'De Vooruitgang' van Gebr. Suurmeyer, Foxhol; 1957, 499g, 201 feet.
The SERTAN's accident in the Manchester Ship Canal could easily have blocked the waterway at its busiest point. On 15th November 1960 the Dutch coaster was entering Eastham Locks whilst bound from Rotterdam to Manchester with general cargo when she hit one of the dolphins which mark the entrance to the canal. The SERTAN was holed, and her pumps could not contain the water. She began to list and sank alongside the canal bank just inside the lock entrance, her crew of 13 taking to her boat - their launching a lifeboat possibly being a unique occurrence in the Ship Canal.

Had she sunk just a few feet to starboard, traffic on the whole canal would have been halted, but SERTAN caused no blockage, which might account for the somewhat leisurely pace of salvage operations. She was righted on the 9th September 1961, but capsized again on 2nd October, although this seems to have been only a temporary set back.

The accompanying photograph was probably taken in September. The salvage vessel alongside is the ADHERANCE, built at Northwich in 1913, and once a coaster owned by James H. Cooper of Widnes.

Once SERTAN was raised, her owners, N.V. van Nievelt, Goudriaan & Co.'s Stoomvaartmaatschappij, lost interest in her, and the wreck was sold to Oslo owners who rebuilt her and renamed her JONETTA. Alas, her new career was to be short: on 13th December 1963 she capsized near Namsos whilst on a voyage from Stavanger to Tromso. *[Roy Fenton collection]*

MARY P. COOPER
Fleming & Ferguson Ltd., Paisley; 1896, 953gt, 194 feet

The early 1960s were a bad time for mishaps in the Mersey; or perhaps just a good period for those who photographed them. Besides the SERTAN and LURCHER, the tug APPLEGARTH tragically sank in January 1960 and the UNITAS hit a buoy and capsized off Seacombe in February 1961. But the most disruption was undoubtedly due to the collision between the MARY P. COOPER owned by William Cooper & Sons Ltd. and the steam coaster FOAMVILLE (869/23) at Stockton Heath in the Manchester Ship Canal on 21st March 1961. The laden sand carrier sank within minutes, her crew of eight jumping into the canal, whilst the FOAMVILLE remained afloat.

Immediately traffic in the upper part of the canal came to a halt, and much of it remained so for a month, several large ships being trapped at Manchester for the duration. One of your editors remembers the aftermath of the collision very well: the disruption on the canal coincided with the Easter school holidays and considerably reduced his opportunities for ship watching. The Ship Canal Company were motivated more by the loss of revenue, and strenuous efforts were made to patch up the old sand carrier and raise her; naval frogmen being employed in the latter stages. Eventually with the help of four large Admiralty salvage pontoons MARY P. COOPER was raised on 11th April and moved to Warrington Wharf: traffic on the canal moving again almost immediately. In the bottom photograph opposite, she has just been raised and is still being pumped out.

Both MARY P. COOPER and FOAMVILLE were broken up soon afterwards. Although the FOAMVILLE was found responsible her owners, John S. Monks & Co. Ltd., did not have to foot the bill, but nevertheless this company - whose ships had attended many salvages - was liquidated soon afterwards.
[This page top: World Ship Photo Library; this page bottom: George Scott collection; opposite page top: Clive Guthrie; opposite page bottom: John Slavin].

ROPNER TRUNK-DECK STEAMERS - PART 2
Harold Appleyard

List of trunk deck steamers built by Ropner (part 2)

Yard number 393 LOWMOOR
O.N. 114429 3976 gt 2560 nt 336.5 x 46.5 x 25.7 feet
T.3-cyl. by Blair and Co. Ltd., Stockton; 294NHP.
8.1902: Completed for W. Runciman and Co., Newcastle.
1919: Sold to the Western Counties Shipping Co. Ltd. (Edwards, Sons and Co. Ltd., managers), Cardiff.
1920: Renamed LOWMEAD.
1922: Sold to F. V. Eberhart and Sons Ltd., London.
1922: Sold to the Polcrest Steam Ship Co. Ltd. (Letricheux and David Ltd., managers), Swansea and renamed NICHOLASTON.
1924: Sold to N. D. Boulgaris, Andros, Greece and renamed DIMITRIOS N. BOULGARIS.
6.6.1933: Arrived at Spezia, Italy for breaking up.

Yard number 399 HERONSPOOL
O.N. 115150 3276 gt 2105 nt 325.0 x 48.1 x 22.9 feet
T.3-cyl. by Blair and Co. Ltd., Stockton; 302NHP.
9.1903: Completed for the Pool Shipping Co. Ltd. (R. Ropner and Co., managers), West Hartlepool.
1916: Managers became Sir R. Ropner and Co.
1928: Sold to B. and J. Koutsoukos, Andros, Greece and renamed EUGENIA M. GOULANDRI.
15.6.1933: Arrived at Spezia, Italy for breaking up.

Yard number 401 TROUTPOOL
O.N. 115158 3281 gt 2110 nt 325.0 x 48.0 x 22.9 feet
T.3-cyl. by Blair and Co. Ltd., Stockton; 302NHP.
11.1903: Completed for the Pool Shipping Co. Ltd. (R. Ropner and Co., managers), West Hartlepool.
1916: Managers became Sir R. Ropner and Co.
30.9.1923: Wrecked south of St. Pierre and Miquelon whilst on a voyage from Las Palmas to St John's, Newfoundland in ballast.

Yard number 402 HARTLEPOOL
O.N. 115162 4409 gt 2872 nt 349.5 x 50.0 x 27.6 feet
T.3-cyl. by Blair and Co. Ltd., Stockton; 371NHP.
1.1904: Completed for the Pool Shipping Co. Ltd. (R. Ropner and Co., managers), West Hartlepool.
1916: Managers became Sir R. Ropner and Co.
1918: Converted to a tanker.
1920: Sold to the Anglo-Saxon Petroleum Co. Ltd., London.
1921: Renamed PURPURA.
27.12.1931: Arrived at Osaka, Japan to be broken up.

Yard number 410 CLARISSA RADCLIFFE
O.N. 119960, 4703 gt 3040 nt 351.5 x 53.1 x 27.6 feet
T.3-cyl. by Blair and Co. Ltd., Stockton; 361NHP
10.1904: Completed for Clarissa Radcliffe Steam Ship Co. Ltd. (Evan Thomas, Radcliffe and Co., managers), Cardiff.
1913: Renamed LLANOVER.
1916: Owners became the Llanover Steam Ship Co. Ltd. (Evan Thomas, Radcliffe and Co, managers), Cardiff.
1917: Owners became the Llangorse Steam Ship Co. Ltd. (Evan Thomas, Radcliffe and Co, managers), Cardiff and renamed LLANGORSE.
1926: Sold to the Britain Steam Ship Co. Ltd. (Watts, Watts and Co. Ltd., managers), London and renamed LALEHAM.
1930: Sold to A.A. Kyrtatas, Andros, Greece and renamed MARIONGA D. THERMIOTIS. Managers subsequently became Goulandris Bros. Ltd., Piraeus, Greece.
1947: Renamed ANTONIOS K.
1949: Sold to Compañia de Navegacion Ponuga Ltda., Panama (J.P. Hadoulis Ltd., London, managers).
25.5.1952: Arrived at Milford Haven to be broken up by T.W.Ward Ltd.

HERONSPOOL, yard number 399.   *[Harold Appleyard collection]*

CLARISSA RADCLIFFE (yard number 410) was illustrated in part one of this article under her original name, but she was to have many others. She is seen in the top photograph under the Greek flag as MARIONGA D. THERMIOTIS, first ship owned by A.A. Kyrtatas. In 1946 she was apparently sold to a company managed in London by the Hadoulis family, but the name ANTONIOS K. and a letter K on her funnel strongly suggests continued Kyrtatas involvement. Although not quite the longest-lived trunk-decker, she survived into the era of aerial photography, and is shown in the bottom photograph under her last name. *[Top: George Scott collection; Bottom: Fotoflite incorporating Skyfotos]*

This fine view of Galveston taken about 1910 shows BURNBY (yard number 415) loading cotton. There is much of interest: the barge and tug traffic, the staging for work on the starboard anchor, the lighter bringing the bales of cotton, and the black longshoremen. Note also the complete lack of mechanisation at this wharf; the cargo is being loaded solely with the aid of two gangplanks and a few trucks. With this angle and lighting, BURNBY's trunk deck is particularly well seen.
[K. O'Donoghue collection]

Yard number 411 SWAINBY
O.N. 106508   3653 gt 2352 nt 325.0 x 48.0 x 26.0 feet
T.3-cyl. by Blair and Co. Ltd., Stockton; 322NHP.
1904: Completed for R. Ropner and Co. West Hartlepool.
22.11.1906: Sank in collision with the British steamer HILLBROOK (3,896/04) off Hartland Point whilst on a voyage from Cardiff to Mauritius with a cargo of coal.

Yard number 415 BURNBY
O.N. 119867   3665 gt 2361 nt 325.0 x 48.1 x 25.9 feet
T.3-cyl. by Blair and Co. Ltd., Stockton; 322NHP.
5.1905: Completed for R. Ropner and Co., West Hartlepool.
1916: Owners became Sir R. Ropner and Co. Ltd.
26.2.1917: Torpedoed and sunk by the German submarine U-39 twenty miles north of Cap Falcone, Algeria, on a voyage from Barry to Algiers with a cargo of coal. The master was taken prisoner.

Yard number 416 BROOKBY
O.N. 119870   3679 gt 2371 nt 325.0 x 48.1 x 25.9 feet
T.3-cyl. by Blair and Co. Ltd., Stockton; 322NHP.
6.1905: Completed for R. Ropner and Co., West Hartlepool.
1916: Owners became Sir R. Ropner and Co. Ltd.
19.6.1917: Torpedoed and sunk by the German submarine U-60 155 miles south by half west of the Fastnet whilst on a voyage from Sagunto to Middlesbrough with a cargo of iron ore.

Yard number 418 STAGPOOL
O.N. 119878   4621 gt 2992 nt 351.5 x 53.1 x 27.6 feet
T.3-cyl. by Blair and Co. Ltd., Stockton; 371NHP.
8.1905: Completed for the Pool Shipping Co. Ltd. (R. Ropner and Co.), West Hartlepool.
1916: Managers became Sir R. Ropner and Co. Ltd.
11.1.1935: Arrived in tow at Rosyth to be broken up by Metal Industries Ltd. having been sold at North Shields for £5,450.
30.1.1935: Demolition commenced.

Yard number 422 TEESPOOL
O.N. 119888   4577 gt 2938 nt 351.5 x 53.0 x 27.6 feet
T.3-cyl. by Blair and Co. Ltd., Stockton; 371NHP.
12.1905: Completed for the Pool Shipping Co. Ltd. (R. Ropner and Co., managers), West Hartlepool.
1916: Managers became Sir R Ropner and Co. Ltd.,
1935: Sold to Branch Nominees Ltd. (E. Atkinson, manager), West Hartlepool for £6,000.
10.1935: Sold to Spanish shipbreakers but sale cancelled.
1936: Sold to Joseph Constantine Steam Ship Line Ltd., Middlesbrough and resold to Metal Industries Ltd. for £6,400 whilst lying in the Tyne under the 'Scrap and Build' scheme.
15.3.1936: Left the Tyne in tow of KINGS CROSS for Rosyth.
1.4.1936: Demolition commenced.

Yard number 426 ROLLESBY
O.N. 119894   3955 gt 2530 nt 350.3 x 50.0 x 24.9 feet
T.3-cyl. by Blair and Co. Ltd., Stockton; 358NHP.
5.1906: Completed for R. Ropner and Co., West Hartlepool.
1916: Owners became Sir R. Ropner and Co. Ltd.
15.9.1917: Torpedoed and sunk by the German submarine U-48 eighty miles east north east of Muckle Flugga whilst on a voyage from Cardiff to Archangel with a cargo of coal.

Yard number 428 MALTBY
O.N. 119898   3977 gt 2540 net 350.0 x 50.0 x 25.0 feet
T.3-cyl. by Blair and Co. Ltd., Stockton; 358NHP.
8.1906: Completed for R. Ropner and Co., West Hartlepool.
1916: Owners became Sir R. Ropner and Co. Ltd.

26.2.1918: Torpedoed and sunk by the German submarine UC-27 ten miles south west by south of Pantellaria whilst on a voyage from Cardiff to Malta with a cargo of coal. Five members of the crew were lost.

Yard number 430 MILLPOOL
O.N. 124317 4218 gt 2707 nt 355.0. x 51.0 x 26.0 feet
T.3-cyl. by Blair and Co. Ltd., Stockton; 369NHP.
10.1906: Completed for the Pool Shipping Co. Ltd. (R. Ropner and Co., managers), West Hartlepool.
1916: Owners became Sir R. Ropner and Co. Ltd.
2.10.1934: Reported in distress and presumed foundered the following day with all hands in position 53.30N by 37.10W whilst on a voyage from Danzig to Montreal with a cargo of rye.

Yard number 433 CLEARPOOL
O.N.124323 4237 gt 2714 nt 355.0. x 51.0 x 26.0 feet
T.3-cyl. by Blair and Co. Ltd., Stockton; 369NHP.
1.1907: Completed for the Pool Shipping Co. Ltd. (R. Ropner and Co., managers), West Hartlepool.
1916: Managers became Sir R. Ropner and Co. Ltd.
12.1933: Whilst lying at North Shields sold to Metal Industries Ltd., Rosyth for about £3,700 for breaking up.
21.12.1933: Arrived at Rosyth.
28.2.1934: Demolition commenced.

Exactly half of the 44 trunk deckers built by Ropners were for their own account. This is their yard number 418, STAGPOOL. (top)
[Harold Appleyard collection]

ROLLESBY, yard number 426 (centre).
[Harold Appleyard collection]

This stern view of MILLPOOL (yard number 430) well illustrates her trunk deck (bottom).
[A. Duncan]

Yard number 436 CARDIGAN
O.N. 123184 4237 gt 2714 nt 355.0 x 51.2 x 26.0 feet
T.3-cyl. by North Eastern Marine Engineering Co. Ltd., Sunderland; 338NHP.
7.1907: Completed for the Cardigan Steam Ship Co. Ltd. (Jenkins Bros., managers), Cardiff.
1914: Sold to N.D. Lykiardopoulo, Argostoli, Greece and renamed ATHANASIOS.
1932: Sold to the Cephalonian Maritime Co. Ltd. (N.D. Lykiardopoulo, manager), Argostoli, Greece.
1938: Sold to Kitagawa Sangyo Kaiun K.K., Osaka, Japan and renamed HOKKO MARU.
20.3.1944: Wrecked at Inubosaki, Honshu, Japan in position 35.42N by 140.53E.

Yard number 437 INGLEBY
O.N. 124339 3815 gt 2313 nt 350.0 x 50.1 x 23.0 feet
T.3-cyl. by Blair and Co. Ltd., Stockton; 301NHP.
8.1907: Completed for R. Ropner and Co., West Hartlepool.
1916: Owners became Sir R. Ropner and Co. Ltd.
1919: Owners became Ropner Shipping Co. Ltd.
1929: Sold to Atlanticos Steam Ship Co. Ltd., Athens, Greece and renamed ATLAS.
13.2.1934: Arrived at Pola, Italy to be broken up.

Yard number 438 COLEBY
O.N. 124274 3824 gt 2320 nt 350.0 x 50.0 x 23.0 feet
T.3-cyl. by Blair and Co. Ltd., Stockton; 301NHP.
9.1907: Completed for R. Ropner and Co., West Hartlepool
27.3.1915: Captured, shelled and sunk by the German auxiliary cruiser KRONPRINZ WILHELM 460 miles north east by half north (true) from Pernambuco whilst on a voyage from Buenos Aires to St. Vincent, Cape Verde for orders with a cargo of wheat.

Yard number 439 THOR
4739 gt 2889 nt 359.9 x 52.5 x 24.7 feet
T.3-cyl. by Blair and Co. Ltd., Stockton; 325NHP, machinery aft.
10.1907: Completed for I/S D/S Thor's Rederi (Wilh Wilhelmsen, manager), Tonsberg, Norway.
1913: Owners became Wilhelmsens D/S A/S (Wilh Wilhelmsen), Tonsberg, Norway.
18.11.1917: Abandoned at sea north west of Hawaii in position 34N by 161W after being overwhelmed in a typhoon whilst on a voyage from San Francisco to Hong Kong with general cargo and steel plates.

Yard number 440 MARGAM ABBEY
O.N. 125092 4471 gt 2778 nt 380.0 x 50.0 x 25.0 feet
T.3-cyl. by Blair and Co. Ltd., Stockton; 320NHP.
11.1907: Completed for Williams and Mordey, Cardiff.
1911: Owners became the Margam Abbey Steam Ship Co. Ltd. (Williams and Mordey, managers), Cardiff.
10.4.1916: Captured and sunk by gunfire from the German submarine U-66 fifty five miles south west quarter south from the Lizard on a voyage from Bordeaux to Barry Roads in ballast.

Yard number 442 ROMANBY
O.N. 127428 3835 gt 2327 nt 350.0 x 50.0 x 23.0 feet
T.3-cyl. by Blair and Co. Ltd., Stockton; 301NHP.
2.1908: Completed for R. Ropner and Co., West Hartlepool.
1916: Owners became Sir R. Ropner and Co. Ltd.
23.12.1917: Sank in collision with the steamer ROMERA (4,949/09) in the North Atlantic in position 47.43N by 10.33W whilst outward bound from Cardiff under sealed orders with a cargo of coal.

Yard number 436 spent most of her life owned by the Lykiardopoulo family under the name ATHANASIOS, as seen here in the Mersey on 20th May 1934. She was built for Jenkins Brothers of Cardiff as CARDIGAN, and along with other later vessels of this type in which the trunk deck was extended for almost the full length of the ship was referred to as a 'bastard trunk', apparently because of their similarity to turret-deckers. During Dr. David Jenkins' researches into the original owners he met a seaman who had served on CARDIGAN and who recalled her as a fine seaworthy ship, but as one unpopular with crews because of the need to manhandle the hatch covers from the trunk deck to the harbour deck before loading, as there was no room to stow them on the upper deck.

Yard number 444 LEEDS CITY
O.N. 123198 4298 gt 2630 nt 355.0 x 51.0 x 26.0 feet
T.3-cyl. by Blair and Co. Ltd., Stockton; 320NHP.
7.1908: Completed for the Instow Steam Ship Co. Ltd. (William Reardon Smith and Son, managers), Cardiff.
1916: Owners became the Bradford Steam Ship Co. Ltd. (William Reardon Smith and Son, managers), Cardiff.
1916: Owners became the St. Just Steam Ship Co. Ltd. (William Reardon Smith and Son, managers), Cardiff.
6.5.1918: Torpedoed and sunk by the German submarine U-86 five miles east by south half south of the Skulmartin Light Vessel whilst on a voyage from Portland, Maine to Manchester with a cargo of flour and wheat.

Yard number 445 BISMARCK
4938 gt 3053 nt 366.0 x 53.0 x 24.9 feet
T.3-cyl. by Blair and Co. Ltd., Stockton; 323NHP.
7.1909: Completed for Chr. Michelsen and Co., Bergen, Norway.
18.11.1909: Exploded and sank whilst loading at Iquique after her cargo of nitrate caught fire.

Yard number 447 GLADSTONE
4927 gt 3088 nt 366.0 x 53.0 x 24.9 feet
T.3-cyl. by Blair and Co. Ltd., Stockton; 325NHP.
9.1909: Completed for Chr. Michelsen and Co., Bergen, Norway.
1914: Sold to N. Suhren, Punta Arenas, Costa Rica, renamed MARINA QUEZADA, and used as a supply ship for German cruisers.
1917: Sold to the Union Sulphur Co., New York, U.S.A. and renamed SEVERANCE.
8.1918 to 3.1919: In use by the Naval Overseas Transportation Service, U.S. Navy as #2063.
1928: Sold to the Diamond Steam Ship Transportation Corporation, Boston, U.S.A.
1941: Sold to Sword Line Inc., New York, U.S.A. and renamed YANKEE SWORD.
1948: Broken up during the third quarter at Philadelphia by Northern Metals Co.

This photograph of INGLEBY (yard number 437) was taken and marketed by H.A. Ebbesen of Aarhus, but there is no sign of the ship flying a courtesy flag when entering a Danish port, although the Ropner houseflag is prominent at the mainmast.
[K. O'Donoghue collection]

COLEBY, yard number 438 (right).
[Harold Appleyard collection]

Note: letters and comments concerning part 1 of this article have been held over and will be printed, together with any on part 2, in the next issue.

FERRY BEYOND THE MERSEY

ROYAL DAFFODIL
R. Stephenson & Co. Ltd., Newcastle-upon-Tyne; 1906, 465gt, 152 feet

Those used to seeing the ferries go about their everyday business on the Mersey tend to assume that these are purely river craft suited only for a very humdrum life. In fact, several Mersey ferries have had eventful lives which have taken them well beyond the confines of the river, and none more so than Wallasey's ROYAL DAFFODIL.

In April 1918, the then plain DAFFODIL and her sister IRIS were enrolled as troop carriers for the daring if perhaps over-ambitious raid on Zeebrugge, aimed at denying German submarines a safe base within easy reach of shipping in the Channel. Although towed to the scene by the cruiser VINDICTIVE, the two ferries took an active part in proceedings once at the Belgian port. For almost an hour, under heavy fire, the DAFFODIL used her engines to keep the VINDICTIVE pinned alongside the mole whilst her troops disembarked. The Mersey ferries got away, but casualties amongst those taking part were heavy. In recognition of valiant service, both ferries were awarded a ROYAL prefix to their name soon after the war.

The twin screw ROYAL DAFFODIL was sold away from the Mersey in 1933 and ran cruises for the New Medway Steam Packet Co. Ltd. between Rochester and Southend: the lower photograph shows her moored on the Medway, perhaps in winter. She was broken up at Ghent, not far from the scene of her wartime exploits, in 1938. *[Bottom: National Maritime Museum N36929]*

ROSE (top), **AN SAORSTAT** (middle) and **BISCOSALVE** (bottom)
J. Jones and Sons, Birkenhead; 1900, 573gt, 156 feet

The exploits of ROSE were not as stirring as those of her one time partner on the Wallasey ferry services, but her service was long and varied. In 1927 the Borough of Wallasey sold her to one Samuel Palmer of Ringaskiddy, who renamed her AN SAORSTAT and used her as a tender for passenger ships calling at Cork: one of no fewer than five former Mersey ferries so employed, including the former ROYAL IRIS. The twin-funnel vessel on the far side of AN SAORSTAT in the accompanying photograph provides an exacting exercise for those *Record* readers who enjoy identification problems.

In 1941 with passenger business at Cork disrupted by the war, Palmer was probably pleased to sell AN SAORSTAT and another of his tenders to the British Iron and Steel Corporation. As BISCOSALVE she was described as a crane ship, and with her superstructure rather crudely cut away her wide open decks would have been useful during salvage work. In 1948 she passed to John Lee of Belfast, and in February 1951 arrived at Preston to be broken up by T.W. Ward Ltd. *[Middle: National Maritime Museum N8759; bottom: WSPL Cochrane collection]*

A LIVERPOOL PROTAGONIST OF SAIL: R.W. LEYLAND AND THE MIGHTY DITTON – PART 1
John Naylon

Ralph Watts Leyland, born in 1842, founded one of Liverpool's last major sailing-ship companies, coming to own some of the largest and best-known vessels of the late nineteenth and early twentieth centuries. Leyland was an enthusiastic advocate of sail for transporting low-value commodities such as grain, coal, nitrate, timber and guano, and persisted with big iron and steel square-riggers while most of his contemporaries were going in for steam. By the late 1880s and early 1890s competition from steam was driving sailing-ship owners into an unceasing search for economies. Leyland's response was to build ever-bigger vessels with high carrying capacity and low running costs which, though little more than floating warehouses, could still extract a reasonable return on investment, especially if combined with careful attention to the pennies of freight rates; small margins on bulk cargoes made all the difference. In his own words: " . . . about the paying capabilities of a large ship - we think the larger the better".

Leylands' golden years

R.W. Leyland and his brother George Richardson Leyland started business in Liverpool as marine insurance brokers in the late 1860s. They began shipowning in 1875 with the purchase of second-hand tonnage, their first vessel being the 682-ton iron barque DOXFORD, followed by the 600-ton iron barque SAN LUIS (1878), the 1,248-ton iron full-rigger NELSON (1880) and the 1,367-ton iron ship GITANA (1881). The brothers' belief in big carriers can be seen in the steady increase in size from their earliest purchases. In 1881 they ordered their first new ship, the 1,819-ton full-rigger GRASSENDALE, named for the family's home village and launched in 1882 by R. Williamson of Workington. With the AIGBURTH of 1882 and the GARSTON of 1883, also built by Williamson, they started the practice of naming their vessels after Liverpool suburbs.

The golden years of the Leyland company were the 1880s and early 1890s. By 1888 R.W. Leyland & Co. were the managing owners of twenty-one big carriers, operated as single-ship companies and constituting one of the largest iron sailing-ship fleets in the United Kingdom. This bold enterprise was built up by the brothers speculating heavily and constantly enlarging their bank overdraft facilities, and yet was controlled by a Liverpool office, in Exchange Buildings, employing as few as seven staff with a combined annual wage bill of little more than £700. This was the hey-day of sail: at the time Leylands were expanding their fleet - say in 1889 - the Liverpool Sailing Ship Owners Mutual Indemnity Association had 1.7 million tons of shipping in its membership.

Decline and fall

In the early 1890s R.W. Leyland's brother George over-speculated and accumulated substantial losses, leading to the break-up of the partnership in 1893. Three years later all the separate single-ship companies were amalgamated into a new firm, The Leyland Shipping Company, but the pressure of change was beginning to tell. By 1897 Leyland himself was acknowledging to his shareholders that his sailing fleet must inevitably give way to steam, that the smaller vessels ought to be sold, and that new tonnage should be steam. Indeed, no new sailers followed the steel ship RIVERSDALE, launched by Hamilton at Port Glasgow in 1894, and in that same year the company built the first of five steamers. By the first decade of the twentieth century the firm was often trading at a loss and paying no dividends - the consequence of depressed freight rates and competition from cheaper German and Scandinavian flags and the subsidised French 'bounty ships'. Ill health forced R.W. Leyland to retire in 1908 and in 1909 management of the company was taken over by J.H. Welsford & Co., also of Liverpool. Welsfords could not make the Leyland sailing vessels pay their way either, and over the next three years the remaining seven ships were sold for a combined total of £27,300. The Leyland Shipping Company was finally dissolved in 1922.

Leylands' three-masters

By the end of the 1880s, as sailing ships grew in size, the four-masted barque had become almost the standard rig for the biggest vessels. Some of the huge later sailers, however, retained the three-masted ship or barque rig, when increasing tonnage would have indicated the addition of a fourth mast. Leylands were the chief adherents of the big three-masted full-rigger, whereas Clyde shipowners and builders in particular regarded them as uneconomical and unhandy, with their lofty masts and tremendous yards. All Leylands' vessels were three-masters, apart from the giant four-poster LIVERPOOL, and twenty out of the twenty-five vessels in the fleet - all those built to Leylands' own account - were full-riggers. The five barques were the smallest, oldest units, all bought second-hand.

The ship that never was

The 1880s and 1890s were a period of great rivalry between British, French and German companies to build ever-larger vessels. In keeping with his philosophy, in 1889 Leyland had his flagship built by Russell & Co. of Port Glasgow. This was the splendid 3,330-ton four-masted iron full-rigger LIVERPOOL,

Leylands' flagship, the four-masted full-rigger LIVERPOOL, in London loading for her maiden voyage to Melbourne in 1889 (top) and at the end of her career on 25th February 1902 (bottom), when she drifted ashore on Alderney in dense fog, two days out on a passage from Antwerp to San Francisco with general cargo. Having cost £23,300, the wreck was sold for £250. *[National Maritime Museum top: P398, bottom: P4403]*

The DITTON's sister-ship SPEKE, at 2,875 gt one of the two largest three-masted full-riggers built in the UK, at anchor in San Francisco (above) and a total loss in Kitty Miller's Bay, Phillip Island on 22nd February 1906 whilst on passage from Sydney Heads to Melbourne (below). Captain Tilton was censured for reckless navigation, having mistaken the Cape Shank light for that on Split Point. *[National Maritime Museum top: P6142, bottom: P6145]*

the largest sailing vessel under the red ensign. In the same year Russells also launched the four-masted full-rigger PETER RICKMERS for Rickmers of Bremerhaven, but constructed of steel and 400 tons smaller than the LIVERPOOL.

It is clear from the correspondence with Russells over the building of the LIVERPOOL that Leyland was contemplating ordering a five-masted sailing ship, which would have been the first in the world, antedating Bordes' barque FRANCE (1), built by D. & W. Henderson of Partick, Glasgow, in 1890, Rickmers' barque MARIA RICKMERS, built by Russells in 1892, and Laeisz' barque POTOSI (1895) and full-rigger PREUSSEN (1902), both built by J.C. Tecklenborg of Geestemunde. Only the volume of work which Russells had on hand, and failure to agree a price, prevented the project from going ahead.

Iron versus steel

Another instance of R.W. Leyland's conservatism, like his preference for the full-rigger, was his choice of iron hulls rather than steel. Steel was already supplanting iron in sailing-ship construction in the 1880s, yet Leyland stuck to iron apart from the steel GARSTON of 1883, the DITTON and SPEKE (1891), the RIVERSDALE (1894) and the wooden KING CEDRIC, built at St. John, New Brunswick in 1874 and owned briefly by Leylands in 1888 and 1889. Perhaps the choice of iron was influenced by Leyland's close association with T.R. Oswald, an outstanding builder of iron sailing vessels.

Leyland's last sailing vessel, the 2,206gt steel ship RIVERSDALE, was built for £17,200 by William Hamilton of Port Glasgow in 1894 - the same year that Workman, Clark built the company's first steamer, the PLANET MERCURY, at Belfast. Here moored off Gravesend on 2nd April 1901, with the Tilbury Hotel in the background, RIVERSDALE ended her days as a barge in British Columbian waters. *[National Maritime Museum G348]*

Leylands' first new ship, the GRASSENDALE, launched in 1882 by Williamson of Workington, had a short life, going missing in 1884 whilst bound for Shanghai from New York. The second GRASSENDALE, pictured here, was also built by Williamson in 1885. R.W. Leyland's son, Ralph junior, made a voyage Hamburg-Melbourne-Falmouth in her in 1898/9 at the tender age of 12, and recorded that she was one of the slowest ships afloat. In 1900 she was sold to G. Granlund of Raumo, Finland, for £10,000 and re-named IMPERATOR ALEXANDER II. She changed hands twice more in Raumo (F. Lehtinen, 1907; N. Panelius, 1917) before going to S. Loftman of Stockholm in 1919, becoming the ERNST. She was lost in the Hertha Flack minefield in April 1920. *[National Maritime Museum P294]*

T.R. Oswald, iron shipbuilder

The earlier vessels which Leylands had built for their own account mostly came from R. Williamson & Son of Workington and Palmers of Jarrow; but after the purchase of the OTTERSPOOL from Palmers in 1884 and the second GRASSENDALE from Williamson in 1885, all subsequent Leyland vessels were built by Oswald, Mordaunt at Southampton and Milford Haven, except for the LIVERPOOL, from Russells, and the very last sailer of the fleet, the RIVERSDALE, built by William Hamilton of Port Glasgow.

Thomas Ridley Oswald, born in 1836 on Teeside, was a nephew of the well-known Sunderland shipbuilder James Laing, in whose yard he worked as an apprentice. He also gained experience helping to construct the GREAT EASTERN at Millwall. In 1857, at the age of 21, he opened his own yard at Pallion, Sunderland, followed by other premises at North Dock, and quickly established a reputation as a builder of iron sailing ships and steamers. However, although he was a prolific builder - launching 149 ships in the space of 16 years at Sunderland - he was less adept at managing his finances. He failed in 1861, again in 1872, and for a third time in 1875, at which point he left the River Wear, dismantling his entire yard and shipping it, together with many of his men, to Woolston, Southampton.

Between 1876 and 1889 Oswald, Mordaunt's Woolston yard (Oswald took John Henry Mordaunt into partnership in 1878) turned out 104 vessels, mostly large iron sailing ships, many of them built for Liverpool owners such as E. Bates & Son, T.R. Williams & Co., H. Fernie & Sons, and J. Coupland. Some at least of these vessels seem to have been designed by Hercules Linton, the designer of the CUTTY SARK. Thomas Oswald, like Leyland, was bold in his vision of how sailing vessels could face steamship competition by turning out ever larger, efficient deadweight carriers; and like Leyland, too, he was an adherent of iron, not building his first steel ship, the screw steamer BENITA, till 1887.

Altogether, Oswald, Mordaunt built eleven vessels for Leyland, beginning with the CRESSINGTON of 1883, which was also the first Leyland ship of over 2,000 tons. In competing for this first order, Oswald was able to quote £1.00 per ton less than Williamson, a significant saving on these big carriers, and indeed Leyland seems to have been able to obtain cheap tenders from Southampton; in the 1880s shipowning and shipbuilding were in depression, and Oswald, Mordaunt were again beset by financial difficulties. The last ship Leyland had built at Southampton was the TOXTETH of 1887, and two years later the yard went into liquidation. The peripatetic Oswald was not quite finished, however. In 1889 he moved to Milford Haven, setting up as the Milford Haven Shipbuilding Co., and although his career as a builder of sailing ships was nearly over, he completed four more notable steel vessels: the Leyland sisters SPEKE and DITTON of 1891, and the four-masted barques LYDERHORN and WINDERMERE of 1892. The Milford Haven yard went into liquidation in 1892 and finally closed in 1895. *[to be continued]*

The 2,595 gt iron full-rigger TOXTETH, launched in 1887 at a cost of £21,800, was the last ship built at Southampton by Oswald, Mordaunt for Leyland. She inaugurated the 'midships bridge or 'Liverpool house' in the Leyland fleet. Although one of Oswald's big carriers, in 1899 she made the best passage of the year from Calcutta to New York, in 99 days. The TOXTETH was one of several sailing vessels to go missing in 1908 on passages around Cape Horn. She left Port Talbot on 2nd March 1908 with 3,906 tons of coal for Tocopilla, in company with Andrew Weir's full-rigger FALKLANDBANK, the British CARNEDD LLEWELLYN and the German ADOLF OBRIG. The Italian barque COGNATI, arriving at Montevideo, reported a lot of wreckage and a number of boats adrift in the ice off the Horn, and the Court of Inquiry into the TOXTETH's disappearance, held in July 1909, concluded that she had probably collided with an iceberg. [National Maritime Museum P6477]

LONG AGO IN LIVERPOOL

The three large sailing vessels in Salthouse Dock have not so far been identified, but all four of the Mersey flats have. To the far left is the sailing flat PRINCE. The other three are Salt Union flats: the steamer PERU of 1881, the sailer NONPAREIL of 1876, and the steam flat DECEMPEDES. The last-named was a quite remarkable vessel; built of steel in 1876 as a sailing flat, she acquired a steam engine in 1888 and an oil engine in 1957, still being registered as late as 1962. The photograph is dated 9th April 1895.
[National Maritime Museum G3615]

This is Langton Graving Docks, sometime prior to 1892. The sheer size of the docks is impressive, with room for one of Liverpool's largest steamers, CITY OF CHICAGO, and some to spare.

The CITY OF CHICAGO (5,202 /83) was built for the Inman and International Steam Ship Co. Ltd. and was lost on 1st July 1892 near the Old Head of Kinsale. The full-rigged ship FRANK PENDLETON (1,414/74), one of the two sailing vessels sharing the left hand dock, was built at Belfast, Maine for the Pendletons of Searsport, Maine. She was unusually large for a wooden ship.

In the background can be seen the London & North Western Railway's Alexandra Dock Station, beyond which is a large obelisk. It is worth noting that the dock and the land around it are no more tidy than they are over a hundred years later. *[National Maritime Museum B8633]*

This view of Langton Number 1 Graving Dock is dated 19th April 1895. Comparison with the previous view shows that the Liverpool Overhead Railway is now in operation: it was opened in 1893. A total of five steamers can be seen, but only the CHERBOURG (1,614/74) can be identified. She was built by J. & G. Thomson at Glasgow for Cunard's Mediterranean service and was broken up in 1909. *[National Maritime Museum G36608]*

Styles in sterns: at least five different fashions can be seen at Langton Dock on 20th April 1895. The small wooden barque to the far right is the GOOD INTENT (410/69), built by Strachan of Montrose for local owners. The ship to her left is the EDWARD D. JEWETT (906/71) also of wood, completed at Portland, New Brunswick. *[National Maritime Museum G3609]*

This time Langton Graving Docks are seen about 1917. All vessels except the Mersey Docks and Harbour Board hopper and the Alexandra tug STALBRIDGE (86/16) are in dazzle paint or grey. The medium-sized, engines-aft vessel is intriguing: can anyone identify her? *[National Maritime Museum N46285]*

Canning Dock and the Liverpool Custom House were photographed sometime between 1882 and 1886. On the left is the iron barque CRAIGNAIR (620/75) from Duncan's Port Glasgow yard. Beyond is the iron OWAIN TUDUR (227/82), the only steamer owned by Parry, Jones and Co. of Liverpool, and which survived until 1929. Alongside OWAIN TUDUR is a Liverpool pilot schooner and beyond, just in front of the Custom House, is what appears to be a steam trawler. On the far right is another product of British North America, the wooden ship MOLILAMO (851/75), built at Chatham, New Brunswick for owners in St. John. *[National Maritime Museum C3132(A)]*

Canning Dock was home to some of Liverpool's few steam trawlers. THISTLE (228/06) was owned by J. Duncan, Son and Co., and had been built by Cochranes at Selby. The clutter on the quay is also of interest: a hand crane and its steam cousin which looks, if anything, slightly smaller, and a boiler bound for Italy. Besides another trawler, the dock also contains one of the ubiquitous Salt Union flats, and a buff-funnelled tug. Yet to receive its coating of soot, the Mersey Docks and Harbour Board building occupies centre stage. The contrast in architectural styles with the warehouses and sail lofts on the dock side could not be stronger. The photograph may have been taken in 1906 as this building was completed in that year, but the Royal Liver Building - completed in 1907 - cannot be seen. [National Maritime Museum P60039]

LOOSE ENDS: TAW SHIPYARDS LTD.

The editors were delighted to be supplied with additional photographs of the Barnstaple shipyard and vessels built there which were not illustrated in Issue 1.

Roger Chapple, who very kindly supplied two of these photographs, also provided a copy of a souvenir booklet produced to mark the launch of the yard's first concrete barge, CRETEPATH. The booklet claimed that building hulls in concrete saved something like 60% of the steel required to construct a conventional ship, and cost about 30% less as well as requiring only unskilled labour. The souvenir pointed out that Barnstaple was ideally suited to concrete shipbuilding with supplies of gravel near by, and looked forward to concrete having an important role in future shipbuilding. Even more ambitiously, it dreamed of ships of 10,000 tons deadweight being built at a down-river extension of the yard. The reality is seen in the aerial view of the yard in the 1930s, with the slipways disused.

Although the seven slipways at the former Taw yard are empty in this 1930s aerial view (left), many features of the shipyard shown on the map in Issue 1 can still be discerned. Just beyond the ways can be seen the river wall which served as a fitting-out berth. On the quay is the track of a narrow gauge railway, although the 40 ton crane has gone. Well back from the edge of the quay can be seen the old plumbers' and fitting shops, now in the yard of the Raleigh Cabinet Works. Immediately inland of the row of slips can be seen another railway, curving round the end of the plater's shed. *[Roger Chapple collection]*

The concrete barge CRETEPATH immediately after her launch into the Taw at Barnstaple on 21st September 1919 (this page, bottom). A few minutes later she ran aground on a sand bank, breaking her back and delaying the launch of the second barge until December. CRETEPATH was blown up in situ. *[Roy Fenton collection]*

Two coasters on the ways at Taw Shipyard with a crowd of workers on what is probably TAW, later PORTHMEOR, the first steamer built at Barnstaple (opposite, middle). She looks a little way off launching, and the adjacent ship, probably GOWERIAN, is still awaiting her propellor. TAW was launched on 29th September 1920 and GOWERIAN a day later. These two slipways are those which can be seen at the bottom of the aerial photograph: they are slightly shorter than the others and do not have a concrete pathway between them. *[Roger Chapple collection]*

A trials photograph of the ANGUS, with name pennant and houseflag (opposite, bottom). She was completed in August 1921 for the Angus Shipping Co. Ltd. of Dundee, managed by Ralph Cowper, but was lost in November of that year. *[National Maritime Museum P2943]*

The CRETEPOND was the second and last concrete barge completed at Barnstaple on 2nd April 1919 (right). Here she is aground near Instow later that year. The size of the barges, which measured 187 feet overall, can be appreciated from the size of the figures by the ladder. CRETEPOND was sunk in 1927 as part of a harbour development. *[National Maritime Museum P27476]*

LOOSE ENDS: KENNETH SHAW - CAPTAIN OWNER

The schooner RYELANDS (above, in Preston Dock) and the ketch IRENE (below) featured in the story of Captain Kenneth Shaw and his ships in Issue 2. Since then, these fine shots have been found. *[WSPL Cochrane and Brownell collections]*

THE BELFAST, MERSEY AND MANCHESTER STEAMSHIP CO. LTD.

Roy Fenton

This is something of a David and Goliath story, with a small but very determined Liverpool shipowning family successfully taking on Belfast's largest and longest-established operator in the short sea trade.

The Mack family deserve to be better known, as for at least a century from the 1870s they had a finger in almost every type of business involving small ships in Liverpool. Beginning in stevedoring work, which involved owning Mersey flats, J.J. Mack and Sons were one of the first Liverpool owners to exploit the new technology of steam in the bulk trades, and from 1881 built up a fleet of steam coasters. In 1887 they were amongst the founders of the Alexandra Towing Co. Ltd., and in 1891 subscribed to the Liverpool and North Wales Steamship Co. Ltd. which operated excursion sailings. Macks maintained an interest in lighterage, and in 1896 were instrumental in forming the Liverpool Lighterage Co. Ltd. and also invested in the United Grain Elevator Co. Ltd. A cargo liner service across the Irish Sea was something they became involved in rather casually, but when the going got tough they persevered with lasting success.

The Belfast and Mersey Steamship Co. Ltd.

In January 1891 the steamer MANCHESTER opened a cargo service between Liverpool and Belfast under the title Belfast and Mersey Steamship Co. Ltd. This was in direct opposition to the Belfast Steamship Co. Ltd., which had been formed in 1852 as the result of Belfast merchants' outrage that steamers from other ports were taking trade felt to be rightly theirs, and had quickly established itself as the dominant operator on the important Belfast and Liverpool route. Owners and managers of the upstart MANCHESTER were Samuel Lawther and Sons of Belfast. Born in 1833, Samuel Lawther was an important Belfast shipowner in his own right, beginning with a fleet of North American-built sailing ships and moving on to large iron and steel sailers. Amongst his other civic and commercial positions, Lawther was a board member of the Belfast Steamship Co. Ltd., and in 1889 had expected to be made its chairman. Instead, the vote went to Thomas Gallaher of the tobacco family, probably because Lawther was felt to be a somewhat pugnacious character, although his credentials as a

MANCHESTER in the Manchester Ship Canal. *[Ambrose Greenway collection]*

shipowner were impeccable. Lawther's bitter disappointment at not being elected saw him denouncing the new chairman as having no knowledge of shipping. His inability to forgive and forget led to his ordering the MANCHESTER from a local shipbuilder to start the rival service to the Belfast Steamship Co. Ltd. To compete MANCHESTER offered freight rates well below those of the established company. In J.J. Mack and Sons, Lawther found willing allies as Liverpool agents, with experience of operating steamers to Belfast and an ability to stand their own ground which exceeded Lawther's. The Belfast Steamship Co. Ltd. responded to the competition by cutting their rates, seriously damaging their own profitability. Worse was to come.

The MANCHESTER's name, and statements from Lawther and the Macks, led Belfast Steamship to expect that a service would be operated from Belfast to Manchester once the Ship Canal was opened in 1894, and to forestall this they began their own service, which proved premature and woefully uneconomic. To rub salt in the wounds, Macks then acquired the 20-year old steamer CALEDONIAN to operate three times each week from Liverpool to Belfast, offering cargo space additional to that of MANCHESTER, plus accommodation for 250 passengers and 300 head of cattle. Again, passenger fares were below those offered by the Belfast Steamship Co. Ltd., forcing them to operate their own cut-price service. Their need for an extra steamer eventually led them to drop the Belfast to Manchester service. In April 1896, the Macks decided that the time was indeed ripe for a Manchester service, and switched the MANCHESTER to this route. Again they proved to have better commercial judgement than the Belfast Steamship Co. Ltd. and the service was so successful that within a few years the YORKSHIRE (394/1893) from Macks' tramping fleet was running alongside MANCHESTER. The service was operated under the title Belfast and Manchester Steamship Company, but no ships were owned under this name.

The CALEDONIAN was old and tired, and no less an authority than W.J. Pirrie of Harland and Wolff offered the opinion that she was scarcely saleable other than for scrap. However, as his company was the main builder to the rival Belfast Steamship Co. Ltd., he was not a totally impartial observer. CALEDONIAN could compete only on price with newer ships on the Belfast to Liverpool service, and was less of a threat than the Belfast and Mersey's earlier efforts to take cargo. Samuel Lawther tired of the fight first, and in 1899 agreed with the Belfast Steamship Co. Ltd. to go to arbitration over the issue of competition. In this, he neglected to consult fully with the Macks. The arbitrators, who do not seem to have been totally independent, decided that the Belfast and Mersey company was hopelessly insolvent, and their award heavily favoured the Belfast Steamship Co. Ltd. The draconian provisions of the arbitration award denied the Macks both their Manchester business and their original coal trade to Belfast. But the Macks were made of much sterner stuff than Lawther, and after direct negotiations with the Belfast Steamship Co. Ltd. had failed to allow them to participate as agents in the Manchester trade, they resorted to legal action to overturn much of the arbitrators' awards. After several setbacks, they eventually succeeded in this, and their perseverance meant that their general cargo service between Belfast and the Mersey continued, with MANCHESTER being helped out by Macks' tramp steamers when required. Macks' CALEDONIAN had been withdrawn in 1900, probably as a goodwill gesture during negotiations, and did not go for scrap as prophesied by Pirrie but crossed the Atlantic to begin a new career under the Brazilian flag. Samuel Lawther retired, dispirited, in 1907 but his son Henry continued to manage the family firm. His other son, Robert, achieved fame as part of Lawther, Latta and Co., managers of the Nitrate Producers' Steamship Co. Ltd.

The Belfast, Mersey and Manchester Steamship Co. Ltd.

The late 1920s saw the Mack family, invigorated by new blood in the shape of Harold and Charles Mack, take a renewed interest in the Belfast trade. As if in preparation, the family firm was incorporated as J.J. Mack and Sons Ltd. in December 1928. In January 1929 the Belfast, Mersey and Manchester Steamship Co. Ltd. was registered. The new company took over the Belfast and Mersey Steamship Co. Ltd. and its shares were split between the Mack family and Henry Lawther.

The registration of the new company was a signal that the Macks were about to exploit another weakness in the services provided by the Belfast Steamship Co. Ltd., whose steamers' tight schedule did not allow for a call at the Woodside lairage on the Birkenhead side of the Mersey and which dealt with much of the livestock imported from Ireland. MANCHESTER was formally transferred to the ownership of the Belfast, Mersey and Manchester Steamship Co. Ltd., as was the steam coaster FLESWICK which was by now the last of Macks' once considerable tramping fleet, and which had been on the Belfast and Mersey berth for some years. In September 1929 a vessel was bought to specifically handle cattle, sheep and pigs. SALTEES of the Clyde Shipping Co. Ltd., the first of several cattle carriers to be bought from the Glasgow company, was renamed STORMONT.

With three ships in service, the company had to work hard to obtain enough traffic. Charles Mack himself was sent out to canvass cargo from such companies as I.C.I. and Shell Mex. And such was the competition that goods were actually moving from Preston to Manchester to be shipped to Belfast; 40 years hence Preston would for a time dominate traffic to Northern Ireland. By today's standards, the ships' schedules seem rather leisurely. In January 1930, for instance, MANCHESTER would load at Pomona Docks on Monday and then sail down the Ship Canal to Liverpool, where she would complete loading and sail for Belfast. Wednesday and Thursday would be spent in Belfast, and on Friday she would discharge in Liverpool, then sail to Manchester and complete unloading there on Saturday. FLESWICK had a similar schedule, but two days behind. STORMONT would load at Manchester on the Friday, although her schedule was made more demanding by the need to unload cattle at Birkenhead and by occasional calls at

FLESWICK at Liverpool. MANCHESTER is ahead of her (above).

STORMONT (1) in the Mersey on 24th September 1930 (below).

Ellesmere Port. Later, calls were made at Bromborough Dock where traffic from Lever Brothers was loaded for Northern Ireland. The FLESWICK tended to be the first of the fleet to be laid up if traffic fell off, although her engines-aft layout and a long hold meant she was the only one suitable for carrying particularly lengthy items of cargo.

In 1933 the MANCHESTER was judged to have reached the end of her days and was broken up, although the company had been receiving enquiries from potential purchasers as late as 1930. Her place was taken by another Clyde cattle boat, RATHLIN, which was renamed GREYPOINT. Replacement of the FLESWICK three years later saw the third cattle carrier arrive, the MOUNTSTEWART (1).

Amalgamation without consolidation

In 1944 the Belfast, Mersey and Manchester Steamship Co. Ltd. became part of the Coast Lines group. Under Alfred Read, this group had bought a very strong stake in the coastal and short sea liner trades round the U.K. Belfast, Mersey and Manchester were considered by Read as a particular prize, although it seems to have taken him at least five years and a number of promises to the Macks to win it. The Belfast Steamship Co. Ltd. had been an early recipient of Coast Line's attentions, and were bought in 1919. But any thoughts by Belfast Steamship's management that the 1944 acquisition spelt the end of competition on the Belfast and Mersey route were short-lived, as Harold Mack negotiated himself a place on the board. He also seems to have had the ear of Alfred Read, who may well have been impressed with the Mack family's business acumen which had so often thwarted the plans of their larger and older rival. At all events, the Belfast, Mersey and Manchester Steamship Co. Ltd. retained a strong measure of independence.

The trio of ships in the Belfast, Mersey and Manchester fleet remained unchanged for ten years, to be broken by the only serious marine accident to affect the company when the STORMONT was in collision with the emigrant carrier EMPIRE BRENT in the Mersey in December 1946. Trying to reach Woodside Landing Stage the inward-bound cattle boat tried to cut across the bows of the passenger ship, which was carrying war brides to Canada. Hit by EMPIRE BRENT's bow, STORMONT turned over on Pluckington Bank as an attempt was made to beach her, but casualties were confined to her cattle. As a temporary measure the WICKLOW was added to the fleet, but within a year she was replaced by yet another Clyde Shipping vessel which became the BROOKMOUNT.

The first attempt by Coast Lines to rationalise their sailings between the Mersey and Belfast came in 1947 when Manchester sailings by the Belfast, Mersey and Manchester company were discontinued. In compensation there were more sailings from Liverpool, Birkenhead and Bromborough, and a second STORMONT arrived from another Coast Lines company to reinforce the fleet.

At frequent intervals the Belfast, Mersey and Manchester ships were replaced, now almost invariably by vessels which had already served other Coast Lines' subsidiaries. The sole exception was the second GREYPOINT, which until 1950 had been FASTNET, yet another of Clyde Shipping's cattle boats. A motor vessel did not arrive until 1955, when it became the first COLEBROOKE, but she was secondhand like every other ship owned by the Belfast, Mersey and Manchester company.

Coast Line's belief that their constituents should continue under their own colours and names remained unshaken until the end of the 1950s, but then some consolidation took place which saw the name Belfast, Mersey and Manchester Steamship Co. Ltd. disappear at the very beginning of 1960. However, rationalisation did not extend too far, and the distinctive ships' names were retained although they were now in the ownership of the Belfast Steamship Co. Ltd., who were thus cheated of complete victory over their old rivals. Indeed, ships transferred to the Belfast and Mersey cattle trade were given time-honoured names COLEBROOKE and STORMONT. Cattle traffic was buoyant, and COLEBROOKE needed to be lengthened in 1962.

The 1960s saw the rise to dominance of unit load and ro-ro traffic, but Coast Lines failure to come to terms with this saw their empire decline rapidly. In the general clearance of conventional tonnage at the end of that decade, the last traces of the Belfast, Mersey

WICKLOW was something of a stop gap, and after only nine months' service with the company was sold for scrap. Her photograph was taken on 19th August 1948: two days later she arrived at Llanelli for breaking up.

BROOKMOUNT (1) (above). *[WSPL]*

Cliff Parson's photo of GREYPOINT (2) on 11th May 1951 (below).*[WSPL]*

and Manchester Steamship Co. Ltd. disappeared as BROOKMOUNT and COLEBROOKE were sold. As cattle carriers, several had lengthy further careers in Middle Eastern waters, some of which were terminated by violence or scuttling. The Belfast, Mersey and Manchester company's erstwhile competitor did not enjoy a much longer life, and the Belfast Steamship's services came to a somewhat ignominious end amidst strikes and recriminations in 1981.

Since the 1970s, Macks' involvement in Liverpool's shipping industry has diminished. The interests of Liverpool Lighterage were absorbed by Alexandra Towing, who themselves have since been sold to Australian owners. In their day, however, a combination of persistence and good commercial judgement had seen the Macks' take on an established and powerful operator, and succeed in capturing and keeping a significant share of its business.

Fleet lists

Belfast and Mersey Steamship Co. Ltd.

MANCHESTER 1918-1929
O.N. 96272 506g 211n 180.7 x 27.5 x 13.2 feet
T. 3-cyl. by McIlwaine and McColl Ltd., Belfast.
3.1.1891: Launched by McIlwaine and McColl Ltd., Belfast (Yard No. 42) for Samuel Lawther and Sons, Belfast as MANCHESTER.
26.1.1891: Completed.
5.1.1918: Owners became the Belfast and Mersey Steamship Co. Ltd. (Samuel Lawther and Sons, managers), Belfast.
23.1.1929: Owners became the Belfast, Mersey and Manchester Steamship Co. Ltd. (John J. Mack and Sons Ltd., managers), Liverpool.
23.6.1933: Arrived at Barrow to be broken up by T.W. Ward Ltd.
14.11.1933: Register closed.

J.J. Mack and Sons

CALEDONIAN 1894-1902 Iron
O.N. 67497 553g 331n 201.0 x 26.1 x 12.9 feet
C. 2-cyl. by John Elder and Co., Govan.
30.4.1874: Launched by John Elder and Co., Govan (Yard No.170) for Robert Henderson Senior, Belfast as CALEDONIAN.
1876: Owner became Robert Henderson Junior, Belfast.
1876: Owner became the Ardrossan Shipping Co., Ardrossan (Robert Henderson and Sons, Belfast, managers).
7.1891: Sold to William Sloan and Co., Glasgow.
7.1894: Acquired by John J. Mack and Sons, Liverpool.
1.2.1902: Sold to William B. Baring (William W. Craig, manager), Liverpool.
4.1902: Sold to Salgado and Co., Rio de Janeiro, Brazil and renamed GUASCA.

5.12.1907: Sunk in collision with a vessel reported to be the Brazilian steamer SAN LOURENCO off Paranagua whilst on a voyage from Paranagua to Santos. Thirty were drowned.

Belfast, Mersey and Manchester Steamship Co. Ltd.

1. **MANCHESTER** 1929-1933
See Belfast and Mersey Steamship Co. Ltd. above.

2. **FLESWICK** 1929-1936
O.N. 102470 647g 195n 179.3 x 28.0 x 11.2 feet
C. 2-cyl. by McKie and Baxter, Glasgow.
16.12.1899: Launched by the Ailsa Shipbuilding Co., Troon (Yard No. 85) for Robert Simpson, Whitehaven as FLESWICK.
17.3.1900: Completed.
18.3.1907: Sold to the Steamship Fleswick Co. Ltd. (John J. Mack and Sons, managers), Liverpool.
1.1.1929: Owners became the Belfast, Mersey and Manchester Steamship Co. Ltd. (John J. Mack and Sons Ltd., managers), Liverpool.
15.10.1936: Sold to Monroe Brothers Ltd., Liverpool.
3.12.1936: Owners became the Kyle Shipping Co. Ltd. (Monroe Brothers, managers), Liverpool.
8.10.1941: Sold to the Culliford Shipping Co. Ltd. (Culliford and Clark Ltd., managers), London.
23.1.1945: Sold to Charles Strubin and Co. Ltd., London.
7.1946: Sold to the Bienvenido Steamship Co. (J. Livanos and Sons, managers), Panama and renamed LEANDROS.
12.2.1949: Foundered north of Corsica whilst on a voyage from Marseilles to Heraklion with a cargo which included carbon disulphide.

STORMONT (1) at Preston in 1936 *[World Ship Photo Library Cochrane Collection]*

3. **STORMONT** (1) 1929-1946
O.N.111176 1077g 459n 250.0 x 35.1 x 16.3 feet
T. 3-cyl. by the Caledon Shipbuilding and Engineering Co. Ltd., Dundee; 14 knots.
25.3.1899: Completed by the Caledon Shipbuilding and Engineering Co. Ltd., Dundee (Yard No. 147) for the Clyde Shipping Co. Ltd., Glasgow as SALTEES.
18.9.1929: Acquired by the Belfast, Mersey and Manchester Steamship Co. Ltd. (John J. Mack and Sons Ltd., managers), Liverpool.
18.10.1929: Renamed STORMONT.
20.11.1946: Capsized and sank off Salisbury Dock, Liverpool following a collision with the steamer EMPIRE BRENT (13,595/25) whilst on a voyage from Belfast to Birkenhead and Liverpool with 220 head of cattle and general cargo.
13.12.1946: After the vessel was cut in two the fore part was raised and placed alongside the river wall at the Albert Dock.
6.2.1947: Register closed.
22.3.1947: Following removal of engines and boilers, the after part was raised.

4. **GREYPOINT** (1) 1933-1950
O.N.121234 1128g 463n 252.2 x 35.1 x 17.1 feet
T. 3-cyl. by William Beardmore and Co. Ltd., Govan.
4.5.1905: Completed by William Beardmore and Co. Ltd., Govan (Yard No. 483) for the Clyde Shipping Co. Ltd., Glasgow as RATHLIN.
20.9.1933: Acquired by the Belfast, Mersey and Manchester Steamship Co. Ltd. (John J. Mack and Sons Ltd., managers), Liverpool.
29.11.1933: Renamed GREYPOINT.
17.3.1950: Smith and Houston Ltd. began demolition at Port Glasgow.
1.5.1950: Register closed.

5. **MOUNTSTEWART** (1) 1936-1949
O.N.124239 1099g 457n 252.3 x 35.7 x 17.0 feet
T. 3-cyl. by Scotts' Shipbuilding and Engineering Co. Ltd., Greenock; 12 knots.
8.11.1907: Completed by Scotts Shipbuilding and Engineering Co. Ltd., Greenock (Yard No. 421) for the Clyde Shipping Co. Ltd., Glasgow as PLADDA.
10.2.1936: Acquired by the Belfast, Mersey and Manchester Steamship Co. Ltd. (John J. Mack and Sons Ltd., managers), Liverpool.
19.3.1936: Renamed MOUNTSTEWART.
30.12.1949: Arrived at Preston to be broken up by T.W. Ward Ltd.
24.2.1950: Register closed.

6. **WICKLOW** 1947-1948
O.N.104963 1032g 414n 260.2 x 34.1 x 15.8 feet
T. 3-cyl. by Blackwood and Gordon, Port Glasgow; 14 knots.
3.5.1895: Completed by Blackwood and Gordon, Port Glasgow (Yard No. 230) for the City of Dublin Steam Packet Co., Dublin as WICKLOW.
20.9.1919: Owners became the British and Irish Steam Packet Co. Ltd., Dublin.
7.7.1920: Renamed LADY WICKLOW.
30.12.1936: Owners became the British and Irish Steam Packet Co. (1936) Ltd., Dublin
15.3.1938: Renamed WICKLOW.
12.11.1947: Acquired by the Belfast, Mersey and Manchester Steamship Co. Ltd. (John J. Mack and Sons Ltd., managers), Liverpool.
21.8.1948: Arrived at Llanelli for breaking up by T. Rees and Co.
31.1.1949: Register closed.

7. **BROOKMOUNT** (1) 1948-1959
O.N.160177 1452g 566n 270.5 x 37.1 x 17.2 feet
T.3-cyl. by D. and W. Henderson and Co. Ltd., Glasgow.
12.7.1927: Launched by D. and W. Henderson and Co. Ltd., Glasgow (Yard No. 787) for the Clyde Shipping Co. Ltd., Glasgow as EDDYSTONE.
15.9.1927: Completed.
1948: Acquired by the Belfast, Mersey and Manchester Steamship Co. Ltd. (John J. Mack and Sons Ltd., managers), Liverpool and renamed BROOKMOUNT.
5.9.1959: Arrived at Barrow for breaking up by T.W. Ward Ltd.

GREYPOINT (1)

MOUNTSTEWART (1) (above)

STORMONT (2) (right). *[World Ship Photo Library]*

8. **STORMONT** (2)/**CAVAN** 1948-1950
O.N.163319 781g 429n 195.0 x 30.7 x 12.4 feet
T.3-cyl. by David Rowan and Co. Ltd., Glasgow.
26.1.1933: Launched by the Burntisland Shipbuilding Co. Ltd., Burntisland (Yard No. 174) for the London and Channel Islands Steamship Co. Ltd. (Cheeswright and Ford, managers), London as LONDON QUEEN.
2.1933: Completed.
1938: Owners became the British Channel Islands Shipping Co. Ltd., London.
1947: Owners became British Channel Traders Ltd., London.
1947: Owners became the Queenship Navigation Ltd., London.
1948: Acquired by the Belfast, Mersey and Manchester Steamship Co. Ltd. (John J. Mack and Sons Ltd., managers), Liverpool and renamed STORMONT.
1950: Renamed CAVAN.
1953: Sold to the Zillah Shipping Co. Ltd. (William A. Savage Ltd., managers), Liverpool and renamed NORTHFIELD.
31.3.1956: Arrived at Preston for breaking up by T.W. Ward Ltd.

9. **GREYPOINT** (2) 1950-1957
O.N.160191 1324g 511n 249.8 x 37.2 x 17.2 feet
T.3-cyl. by the Caledon Shipbuilding and Engineering Co. Ltd., Dundee.
2.1928: Completed by the Caledon Shipbuilding and Engineering Co. Ltd., Dundee (Yard No. 315) for the Clyde Shipping Co. Ltd., Glasgow as FASTNET.
1950: Acquired by the Belfast, Mersey and Manchester Steamship Co. Ltd. (John J. Mack and Sons Ltd., managers), Liverpool and renamed GREYPOINT.
28.8.1957: Arrived at Preston for breaking up by T.W. Ward Ltd.

10. **MOUNTSTEWART** (2) 1950-1955
O.N.143620 1097g 506n 240.0 x 36.2 x 16.2 feet
T. 3-cyl. by A. and J. Inglis Ltd., Glasgow.
3.1920: Completed by Harland and Wolff Ltd., Glasgow (Yard No. 592G) for Coast Lines Ltd., Liverpool as SOMERSET COAST.
1950: Acquired by the Belfast, Mersey and Manchester Steamship Co. Ltd. (John J. Mack and Sons Ltd., managers), Liverpool and renamed MOUNTSTEWART.
16.11.1955: Arrived at Troon for breaking up by the West of Scotland Shipbreaking Co. Ltd.

MOUNTSTEWART (2) (above). *[Keith Byass]*

COLEBROOKE (1) in Clarence Dock, Liverpool in August 1959, shortly before transfer to William Sloan (below). *[World Ship Photo Library]*

11. **COLEBROOKE** (1) 1955-1959
O.N.168858 869g 424n 234.5 x 35.2 x 11.7 feet
Oil engine 2S.C.S.A. 8-cyl. by British Auxiliaries Ltd., Glasgow.
6.1943: Completed by Ardrossan Dockyard Ltd., Ardrossan (Yard No. 391) for Coast Lines Ltd., Liverpool as SOUTHERN COAST.
11.1955: Acquired by the Belfast, Mersey and Manchester Steamship Co. Ltd. (John J. Mack and Sons Ltd., managers), Liverpool and renamed COLEBROOKE.
10.1959: Owners became William Sloan and Co., Glasgow and renamed FORTH.
1962: Owners became the British Channel Islands Shipping Co. Ltd., London and renamed SOUTHERN COAST.
1967: Sold to D. Varverakis and Chr. Hadjigeorgiou, Piraeus, Greece and renamed ELEISTRIA.
1979: Sold to Al Rubayia Transport Co., Panama and renamed AL RUBAYIA.
1979: Sold to Naviglory Ship Corporation, Panama.
1985: Sold to the Al-Rubayah Live Stock Trading and Transportation Co.
27.6.1985: Sprang a leak and sank in heavy weather at Bombay in position 18.57.30N by 72.51.24E. She had been laid up at Bombay since 12.1.1983. Subsequently raised and sold to the Agra Steel Corporation, Mumbai, and broken up by 6.1986.

MOUNTSTEWART (3) (right).
[K. Cunnington]

BROOKMOUNT (2) arriving at Preston (below).

12. **MOUNTSTEWART** (3)   1957-1960
O.N.187106   892g   376n   224.5 x 36.2 x 13.7 feet
Sulzer type oil engines 2S.C.S.A. 8-cyl. by G. Clark (1938) Ltd., Sunderland.
24.3.1955: Launched by the Ardrossan Dockyard Ltd., Ardrossan (Yard No.417).
7.1955: Completed for Coast Lines Ltd., Liverpool as ESSEX COAST.
6.1957: Acquired by the Belfast, Mersey and Manchester Steamship Co. Ltd. (John J. Mack and Sons Ltd., managers), Liverpool and renamed MOUNTSTEWART.
1.1.1960: Owners became the Belfast Steamship Co. Ltd., Belfast.
1965: Owners became Coast Lines Ltd., Liverpool.
1967: Owners became the British Channel Islands Shipping Co. Ltd., London.
1969: Sold to the Greek Current Producers Line of Panama, Panama and renamed EVDELOS.
1971: Sold by order of the Admiralty Marshall to Pounds Shipowners and Shipbreakers Ltd., Portsmouth, after lying at Shoreham for a year.
1972: Sold to Pothitos Shipping Cia. S.A., Somali Republic and renamed MICHALIS.
1972: Owners became Pothitos Shipping Co., Panama.
1975: Sold to the Mossel Bay Shipping Co. Ltd., Panama.
1976: Sold to the Proodos Shipping Co. Ltd., Piraeus, Greece and renamed PROODOS.
1979: Sold to Maritime Commission Inc., Panama and renamed MANUEL.
5.1986: Arrived at Salamina, Greece to be broken up.

13. **BROOKMOUNT** (2)   1960-1970
O.N. 182122   995g   438n   264.6 x 38.7 x 12.5 feet
Sulzer oil engines 2S.C.S.A. 8-cyl. by William Denny and Bros. Ltd., Dumbarton.
8.1949: Completed by William Denny and Bros. Ltd., Dumbarton (Yard No.1434) for Burns and Laird Lines Ltd., Glasgow as LAIRDS BEN.
9.1959: Acquired by the Belfast, Mersey and Manchester Steamship Co. Ltd. (John J. Mack and Sons Ltd., managers), Liverpool and renamed BROOKMOUNT.
1.1.1960: Owners became the Belfast Steamship Co. Ltd., Belfast.
1970: Sold to Compania Naviera Vivi S.A., Panama and renamed IKARIA.
1971: Sold to Rosade Lines S.A.L., Beirut, Lebanon and renamed PIERRE RODOLPHE.
1973: Sold to Khodr Adel El-Hoss, Beirut and renamed ZIAD.
1979: Renamed SWEET WAVES.
19.11.1983: Sank after being shelled during the Lebanese Civil War whilst laid up at Tripoli, Lebanon.

COLEBROOKE (2) at Liverpool 29th July 1960 (right). [F.W. Hawks]

STORMONT (3) in the Mersey, in William Sloan's funnel colours (below).

14. **COLEBROOKE** (2) 1960-1970
O.N.182101 990g 437n 264.0 x 38.7 x 12.5 feet
1963: 1,075g 494n 286.0 x 38.7 x 12.5 feet
Oil engine 2S.C.S.A. 8-cyl. by Sulzer Brothers Ltd., Winterthur.
11.1948: Completed by William Denny and Bros. Ltd., Dumbarton (Yard No.1416) for Burns and Laird Lines Ltd., Glasgow as LAIRDS MOOR.
3.1960: Acquired by the Belfast Steamship Co. Ltd., Belfast and renamed COLEBROOKE.
1963: Lengthened by Grayson, Rollo and Clover Ltd. at Birkenhead.
1970: Sold to Losinjska Plovidba, Rijeka, Yugoslavia and renamed MIRNA.
1975: Owners became Losinjska Plovidba OOUR Brodarstvo, Rijeka.
1.12.1984: Scuttled off Nerezine, Mali Losinj, Yugoslavia.

15. **STORMONT** (3) 1963-1965
O.N.185507 906g 344n 226.5 x 35.7 x 13.1 feet
Oil engines 2S.C.S.A. 8-cyl. by George Clark (1938) Ltd., Sunderland.

20.9.1954: Launched by George Brown and Co. (Marine) Ltd., Greenock (Yard No.260) for Coast Lines Ltd., Liverpool as FIFE COAST.
12.1954: Completed.
20.6.1958: Owners became William Sloan and Co., Glasgow and renamed FRUIN.
24.12.1963: Acquired by the Belfast Steamship Co. Ltd., Belfast and renamed STORMONT.
10.1965: Owners became Coast Lines Ltd., Liverpool.
13.12.1966: Owners became the Tyne-Tees Steam Shipping Co. Ltd., Newcastle-upon-Tyne.
1.10.1971: Managers became P. & O. Short Sea Shipping Ltd.
31.3.1975: Managers became P. & O. Ferries.
16.7.1976: Owners became P. and O. Ferries (General European) Ltd., Liverpool.
14.10.1976: Sold to Farouk Rassem W. Moukahal and Ahmad Hassan Zeido (Union Commercial Co., managers), Beirut, Lebanon and renamed RABUNION VII.
1992: Sold to Baraa Z Shipping Co. S.A.R.L., Beirut, Lebanon (Zeido Hassan Zeido, Aleppo, Syria, manager) and renamed BARAA Z.
1994: Broken up at Tripoli, Lebanon.

PUTTING THE RECORD STRAIGHT

Letters, additions, amendments and photographs relating to articles are welcomed. Letters may be lightly edited for inclusion.

One for the Goolies
I enjoyed the article on Goole Colliers by Roy Fenton in Issue 2 very much. Being a "Goolie" by birth, I drooled at the superb photographs. It has always amazed me how these colliers kept running for so long in view of the treacherous, winding and fast flowing River Ouse that they had to negotiate on every voyage, in an age when navigational aids were not what they are today. Mention was made in the article that the RALPH CREYKE of 1879 lasted until she was eventually lost in 1912. She certainly had many near scrapes whilst on service before this date, the notable ones being listed below.

January 1885: Whilst arriving at Goole from Ghent with general cargo she attempted to swing in the river, as most ships do when entering the Port of Goole. On this occasion her broadside amidships swung into the stern of the steamer CONTEST which was at anchor in the river waiting to enter the port having arrived from London with general cargo. The RALPH CREYKE sustained a large "hole" stretching from her decks to below the water line and she had to make a speedy entrance to the port to effect repairs.

June 1887: This time as the RALPH CREYKE approached Goole she found a keel laying across her course to the dock entrance and so, to avoid running the keel down, she collided, rather violently it was reported, with the quay wall. The outcome was that her bow was seriously damaged, several plates being broken.

November 1888: As the RALPH CREYKE departed from Goole for Antwerp with general cargo she collided with the CUXHAVEN which was swinging in the river after arriving from Hamburg. The RALPH CREYKE was badly damaged on the port side having railings and bulwarks smashed, a portion of which was said to have been carried away on the stern of the CUXHAVEN! The RALPH CREYKE's plates were also bent, the lifeboat smashed and one of the davits broken. She had to put back into Goole for repairs.

Of the other vessels mentioned in the article, the ALTONA also had problems when approaching Goole. On 13th August 1908 she was inward bound with general cargo from Delfzijl in Holland and in order that she did not run into a string of keels towed by a tug, it was decided to run her ashore on to the training wall on the south bank of the Ouse between Swinefleet and Goole. The bank is very steep here and she went well up the bank so that when the tide fell she was left with her stern in the water but with her bow up the steep bank. It was feared at one time that she might heel over but luck was with her and she refloated safely on the evening tide.

We frequently read of mishaps that occur at sea but often the ones that happen on our inland rivers go unrecorded.
ROY CRESSEY, 12, Templestowe Drive, Whitkirk, Leeds LS15 7BR

In a future issue we hope to publish an article by Roy on accidents in the Ouse.

Even heavier lifts
I noticed a slight error in the information given on heavy lift ships in Issue 2. On page 98 it was stated that the previous greatest capacity of the Strick Line ships was the 85 ton traditional rig on the BALUCHISTAN. This is not strictly correct as there were two ships with greater capacity: the steamers NIGARISTAN (5) of 1947, SWL 110 tons; and TABARISTAN (6) also of 1947, SWL 150 tons. Many thanks for a fascinating publication.
DOUGLAS YATES, 65 Jones Lane, Hythe, Southampton SO45 6AW.

Gin and derricks
Many congratulations on the second number of *Ships in Focus RECORD*. I was particularly interested in the article on the Goole steamers. From memory the Goole fleet ran liner services to the near-Continent and the Baltic, and there are pictures in the Town Docks Museum of ships with deck cargoes of threshing machines for Russia made by Fosters in Lincoln. The use of what might be termed topmast derricks was, I thought, dictated by the rise and fall of the tide at Riverside Quay in Hull where a derrick boom in the conventional position would be unworkable. There is a good model of the OUSE in the Town Docks Museum. We borrowed her from the National Railway Museum and built a section of Riverside Quay for her to lie against. She is complete with topmast derricks and gin blocks.
EDWARD W. PAGET-TOMLINSON, Easton House, Pound Lane, Easton, Wells, Somerset BA5 1EF.

ALTONA ashore in the Ouse in August 1908: see letter above. *[World Ship Photo Library]*

ELLOUGHTON docking at Preston (see letter from W.D. Phillips).

Phillips on Phillips
In his splendid article about the coasters built at the Taw shipyard Roy Fenton's notes about ENID MARY mentioned JOHN SHAW as the only other vessel owned by W.A. Phillips. However, my records indicate that they also owned ELLOUGHTON (954/19) from 1930 until 1935. She was sold to W.S. Kennaugh & Co. in the latter year and became BIRKER FORCE. She was one of their last vessels when she arrived at Blyth on 29th January 1959 to be broken up. Her previous owners had been W.A. Jenkins & Co. In 1934 William A. Phillips became W.A. Phillips & Sons Ltd.
W.D. PHILLIPS, Coppers End, Frogmore, near Kingsbridge, Devon TQ7 2NU.

Hello ULOOLOO
For the Record, I note that the steamship behind the armed trawler KOROWA on page 79 is the ULOOLOO of 3,236 gt. She was built by Beardmore in 1924 and served the Adelaide Steamship Company Ltd. until 1957. A ulooloo (or should it be an ulooloo) is the aboriginal word for a billabong which never dries.

Apparently ULOOLOO did 11 knots on 31 tons of coal. It must have been hot work down under. She was sold to Hong Kong becoming CLYDE BREEZE and finally HANKONG before being scrapped there in 1962.
JOHN BARTLETT, 6 Cottenham Park Road, London SW20 0RZ

Australasian amendments
MORETON BAY (Fleet in Focus: Aberdeen and Commmonwealth Line) was not requisitioned by the Australian Government in 1939, but by the British Admiralty. The same applies to ESPERANCE BAY.

I cannot understand the apostrophe in HOBSONS' BAY. There was none as the name was painted on the ship, nor in Lloyd's Register, nor is there any in the name of the bay after which the ship was named. There is no mystery about this ship's 1936 name change. It was carried out at the request of the Worker's Travel Association which used to charter the previous ESPERANCE BAY and told the company it wished to carry on chartering a ship with the same name.

The map in the article on the KAIPARA grounding is anachronistic - the harbour bridge was not completed until 1959. Further, the term 'docks' is unknown in the New Zealand context: a more appropriate description on the map might have been 'city wharves.' The KAIPARA was built in 1903, not 1906.

The date of the DUQUESNE grounding was 5th November 1889. The vessel referred to as MARERO was in fact Tyser Line's MARERE. The Union Steam Ship Company have owned only one ship named WAIMATE and she was not built until 1951. The vessel concerned in the 1904 incident was the New Zealand Shipping Company's WAIMATE of 1896. The reference to the DORSET's grounding is out of time order. Between her building and the KAIPARA grounding she made only two visits to Auckland, arriving from London on 6th April 1906 and again on 20th November that year, so the WAIMATE's grounding cannot be the last.

On page 128 the photo shows the first *steamer* named HURUNUI. The first New Zealand Shipping Co. use of this name was for a sailing vessel built in 1875. Another feature distinguishing the HURUNUI from the 1906-1908 built O class was that the latter had cranes at number 3 hatch whilst the HURUNUI had kingposts.

BILL LAXON, Waimarana, Upper Whangateau Road, PO Box 171, Matakana 1240, New Zealand.

John Hill points out that the groundings in Auckland harbour were reported in the order they appeared in the minutes of the Enquiry. The map was only intended to give those unfamiliar with the location an indication of where the accident took place.

Lowestoft and its railway tugs

I have just caught up with *Ships in Focus RECORD* Issue 1 and the fascinating article on the Lowestoft tugs. This piece is not only most interesting but also fills many gaps in my own knowledge and archives. From my own records, much of which are derived from official registration documents, I can supplement some details.

RAINBOW. Registration documents give builder as J. Ash, Cubitt Town. I suspect that J. Stewart subcontracted the hull, supplying only the engine themselves.
RESOLUTE was scrapped in 1936 by T.W. Ward at Grays, Essex.
IMPERIAL (2). Her 1883 engine was 1-cyl half beam.
VICTOR. She was built in 1876 by Alexander Pratt at Firhill, Glasgow, possibly for his own account. The Pratt family seem to have been shipbuilders in both Glasgow and Poplar, later living at Forest Gate.
1879: Fitted with new 2-cyl. compound engine by J. Stewart and Son, Blackwall; 35 NHP.
13.3.1896: Sold to Joseph Constant, London.
4.5.1898: Sold to Alfred Tolhurst, Northfleet.
5.10.1898: Sold to Phillip Margetts, Canning Town.
8.12.1899: Owner became George Margetts.
2.12.1906: Owner became W.J. and S. Margetts.
19.12.1916: Sold to the Grimsby Steam Tug and Launch Co. Ltd., Grimsby.
9.4.1918: Worn out and condemned as a constructive total loss.

The Lowestoft tug MAY. *[National Maritime Museum P27468]*

MAY. Registry closed and sold for scrap in 1923.
QUEEN. Original engine was a 2-cyl. high pressure.
LOWESTOFT. There is a note that her owners applied in 1954 to transfer her to V. van der Bossche, Boom, Belgium for scrap, but perhaps approval was not given.
BARTON had two 2-cyl. engines.
NESS POINT was yard number 289.
DAVID ASPREY, 60 Barnstaple Road, Thorpe Bay, Southend-on-Sea, Essex SS1 3PA.

Jerzy Swieszkowski, author of the article, writes that the Great Eastern Railway minutes refer to RAINBOW as ordered from J. Stewart, and he received all payments recorded, but it is quite likely that Stewart subcontracted the hull to Ash. MAY is poorly documented in railway minutes; Jerzy was told that she was actually broken up by Seago at Yarmouth in 1930, but there is no proof. Jerzy has a photograph which confirms LOWESTOFT was broken up at Lowestoft.

A voyage too many
I especially enjoyed the article on the "Bay Boats" as I had sailed on the MORETON BAY, and on the nightmare final voyage of the LARGS BAY (January 1957). It should have been a four-month trip, but took six months and three weeks. We were three months on the Aussie coast, caught fire in Melbourne and were towed into Fremantle. Homeward bound, we were towed into Durban where we spent a month on repairs (and blew our pay-offs). As she was 36 years old with clapped-out engines and generators it's no wonder. She was constantly breaking down and was completely without power (no lighting even). Out of potatoes, we settled for rice-cakes as our vegetables. Except for the war years, she made 91 Aussie voyages and steamed three million miles. Guess she made one trip too many!
D. COOPER, 47 Russell Close, Bexleyheath, Kent DA7 4HX

Points from Issue 2
The split superstructure (page 114) was a common practice in passenger liners. It was a feature of Nelson Line's Highland ships and Royal Mail S.P. Co.'s ships amongst others. It was referred to as the "Chastity Belt" because the officers lived in the island bridge housing and were only allowed into the passenger accommodation during certain specified hours. The Master at Arms and his staff patrolled the passenger alleyways. Several of the post-First World War Anchor, Cunard and White Star liners also had this hatch abaft the bridge. On the old coal burning liners and cargo vessels this hatch had a practical purpose: it gave access to the bunker spaces or a bunker hatch would be situated immediately between it and the funnel (I imagine that, usually, the hatch derricks also served the bunker hatch if necessary).

On the subject of coal (Goole colliers, page 119) the blocks hanging from the yards of the ALTONA and the ALT were for discharging the cargo. The winches would be set to run at a set speed and there would be a gang for each barrel end. The derrick or boom was plumbed above the bulwarks and a rope rove through the block was used to drag the coal skip up the side of the hatch and swing it over the coaming to the top of a chute down which the coal was tipped into the waiting wagon on the quay. Grab cranes were not in general use in those days. This method of discharge was still in use in Hull docks in the 1960s. I can remember discharging palm kernels and ground nuts from West Africa to barges in this way.

My ship was alongside in Dundee in January 1963 when BENARTY was fitting out. This may be apocryphal, but we were told that the accommodation block of the BENARTY was lifted into position by the Stülcken derrick, killing two birds with one stone as this served as the derrick's test load!

Alan McClelland mentions Mr. E.H. Watts of the Britain Steamship Co. Ltd. His views on tramp ship design were certainly unconventional. I can remember, as Stevedore Superintendent, loading the WIMBLEDON. This was one of two sisters and these were, I think, the last ships built for the company. Apart from the problem of loading a general cargo into a vessel designed for tramping, mainly caused by the derrick and hatch arrangement, night work meant a sleepless night for most of the crew as three hatchways were trunked up to the uppermost deck with the officers' accommodation on the other side of the trunking on the port side and the crew's on the starboard. Every time a piece of cargo or the derrick hook struck the bulkhead, virtually the whole crew was woken up. The accommodation was of a very high standard, however. There were galleries on either side similar to a passenger liner. The cabins opened off these galleries on the inboard side and were, thus, only the thickness of the bulkhead from the hatch trunking. These two ships also had an island bridge where the Captain and Senior Mate's accommodation was situated. The Chief and Second Engineer's cabins were, I think, around the funnel casing, aft.

The standard to the photographs in this edition is superb. Keep up the good work.
G. HOLMES, MNI, 17 Bayswater Court, Newport Avenue, Wallasey, Wirral, Cheshire L45 8QJ.

WIMBLEDON and WEYBRIDGE were built for Watts, Watts in 1958; but their last newbuilding was the WILLESDEN of 1961.

More points from Issue 2
An oft occurring error appears in the description of the machinery of the Aberdeen & Commonwealth Line "Bay boats". It is not really correct to say that the ships were propelled by two steam turbines. You could, perhaps, refer to two steam turbine sets. The ships actually had four steam turbines, a high pressure turbine and a low pressure turbine driving each propeller shaft.

The interesting story about heavy lift ships might have pointed out that, apart from the spectacular booms and deck equipment, the ships were generally equipped with large, sophisticated, remotely-controlled winches. The winches were usually installed in the 'tween decks and, in the case of the Stülcken derricks, they were usually controlled from platforms high up the masts. To maintain stability, and to control the angle of heel, most ships had dedicated ballast tanks. Fuel and ballast pumps had extra large capacity, and were controlled by means of auto-recording inclinometers. Some of the smaller heavy-lift ships were actually fitted with extending arms, so that the ships could literally lean on the quay when picking up heavy loads. Whilst Paul Boot rightly praises the Stülcken, it should be mentioned that the idea was conceived by a Hansa Line officer and developed jointly by Hansa and Stülcken, in 1953-54. The H.C. Stülcken Sohn shipyard was much occupied in building warships for the German Navy, but unfortunately it encountered financial difficulties and the shipyard, together with the Stülcken mast patent, were taken over by Blohm & Voss, Hamburg, in February 1966.

Whilst it is quite correct that the NORTHWOOD and other Constantine vessels mentioned in the Skyfotos feature could be described as colliers, they were unusual, because they invariably returned to the Tyne with cement cargoes from the Thames. The cement was for the Cement Marketing Co. and was discharged at Johnson's Quay, Gateshead.

The photograph of the BALANTIA reminded me of happy days. She was one of seven Libertys allocated to Royal Mail Lines for management. After the War, four of them were retained and renamed BALANTIA, BERBICE,

BERESINA and BARRANCA (traditional Royal Mail river names). The ships ran mainly from the U.K. to Brazil and the River Plate. It is interesting to note the erection on the port side of the after mast of the BALANTIA. This would be cattle or horse pens. Pedigree bulls and horses were frequently transported from the Thames to South America aboard Royal Mail ships. The deck erections, though stoutly built, were temporary and were dismantled after use. Sometimes the livestock were tended by a cattle man, who signed on for the voyage. Otherwise, the bosun or the apprentices tended to the animals - and sometimes received a gratuity!

JOHN B. HILL, The Hollies, Wall, Hexham, Northumberland NE46 4EQ

The caption to the HAMPTON FERRY on page 108 of Issue 2 described the gantry fitted in 1944 to allow locomotives and rolling stock to be unloaded on normal quaysides. Its size can be appreciated from this view of HAMPTON FERRY in Dover during 1946. *[National Maritime Museum P34784]*

Sources and Acknowledgements

Photographs are from the collection of John Clarkson unless otherwise credited. We thank all who gave permission for their photographs to be used, and are particularly grateful to Fred Hawks, Mike MacDonald, Kevin O'Donoghue, George Scott, and John Slavin; to Tony Smith, Cliff Parsons and Keith Byass of the World Ship Photo Library; and to the museums and institutions listed for help in finding photographs.

In researching captions, sources have included *Lloyd's Register, Lloyd's Confidential Index, Lloyd's War Losses, Mercantile Navy Lists, Marine News* and Closed Registers (Class BT110) in the Public Records Office. Use of the facilities of the World Ship Society's Central Record and of Lloyd's Register of Shipping are gratefully acknowledged.

Yeoward Line
An account of the first century of Yeoward Brothers appears in *Sunward by Yeoward* by Theodore W.S. Barry (Granta Editions, Cambridge; 1994). *Nightmare Convoy* by Paul Lund and Harry Ludnam is the story of convoy OG71 and the loss of AGUILA (2). OG71 is also reflected in *The Cruel Sea* by Nicholas Montserrat who was present as an officer on board HMS CAMPANULA.

A class of three
Cheshire County Archives, *Lloyd's Weekly Casualty Reports*, 'Tugs and Towage News' by M.J.Gaston and 'Reas of Liverpool' by W.B. Hallam, both in *Sea Breezes;* John Bartlett, Bill Harvey, Alan Phipps, Mr. G.Robinson Assistant Dock Manager Hull, and Captain V. Thomas.

Mersey Mishaps
Casualty information came from *Lloyd's Weekly Casualty Reports.* Thanks to Clive Guthrie for researching certain of these.

Ferry beyond the Mersey
West Coast Steamers by L.D. Duckworth and G.E. Langmuir (T. Stephenson & Sons Ltd., Prescot; 1966) and *Irish Passenger Steamship Services* by D.B. Neill (David & Charles, Newton Abbot, 1971) were referred to. Thanks also to Harry Hignett.

A Liverpool protagonist of sail
A detailed history of the Leyland company is provided by David Walker, *Champion of Sail: R.W. Leyland and his Shipping Line* (Conway Maritime Press, London; 1986). Commander R. Leyland (R.W. Leyland's son) gives an insider's view of the company's management in "The Leyland Line of Liverpool", *Sea Breezes* (New Series), Vol.XIV, July-December 1952, pp.266-76. A list of the Leyland sailing vessels appears in *Sea Breezes* (Old Series), Vol.XVIII, February-October 1934, pp.144-5, 176-7. The career of T.R. Oswald is described in Adrian B. Rance, *Shipbuilding in Victorian Southampton* (Southampton University Industrial Archaeology Group, Southampton; 1981) and in J.W. Smith and T.S. Holden, *Where Ships are Born: Sunderland 1346-1946: A History of Shipbuilding on the River Wear* (Thomas Reed, Sunderland; 1946).

The Belfast, Mersey and Manchester Steamship Co. Ltd.
Across the Irish Sea by Robert Sinclair (Conway Maritime Press, London; 1994) proved very useful and *The Nitrate Boats* by David Burrell (World Ship Society, Kendal; 1995) gave details of the Lawthers. Thanks also to Paul Mack and Anne Cowne.

CW01334342

THE
LIFE
OF
TWINS

Insights from over 120 Twins, Friends and Family

By K&E, founders of Twinning Store

INSPIRATION BY THE COAST

Los Angeles, 2019

Copyright © 2019 K&E - All rights reserved.

No part of this publication may be reproduced, distributed, or transmitted in any form or by any means, including photocopying, recording, or other electronic or mechanical methods, or by any information storage and retrieval system without the prior written permission of the publisher, except in the case of very brief quotations embodied in critical reviews and certain other noncommercial uses permitted by copyright law.

Illustrations by K&E//Twinning Store

Library of Congress Cataloging-In-Publication Data

Names: K&E (founders of Twinning Store)

Title: The Life of Twins - 120 Insights from over twins, friends and family / K&E

Description: Los Angeles, Inspiration by The Coast, 2019

ISBN: 9781676195405

To our parents:

Thank you for always supporting our ambitions and always reminding us to be grateful for each other.

#twinfluencer:

Without you, this book would not be possible. You help us grow and you inspire us every single day.

Introduction	11
1 Who are we and why we are writing this book	13
Why read this book?	15
How to read this book	16
2 Being called the twins	19
Twin nicknames	21
How to say the word twin	22
3 Perks of being twins	25
Hannah & Jess Gerlacher	28
Lucy Knott & Kelly Sharpe	28
Megan & Liz	29
Bud & Aidan Brenna Williams	29
Lisa Marie Elwes & Janet Kurbikoff	30
Chloé & Francesca Townsend	30
Eric Niyomwungere & Aimable Niyongabo	31
Kevin & Chris Delgado	31
Charlotte & Heather Howard	32
Julia and Michael Toronczak	32
Albert & Robert Gomez	33
Alexis & Samantha Belbel	33
4 Downsides to being twins	35
Jennifer & Ashley Rubin	38
Destiny Mitchell & Alexxus Mitchell	39
Rachel & Rebekah Aladdin (aka Reine)	39
Milena & Jelena Aleksic	40
Annette Schreyer & Birgitte Schreyer Duarte	41
Carmen & Camille Thomas	42
5 Common twin questions	43
Stephanie Dickinson	46
David & Fidel Solorzano	46
Jessica & Stephanie	46

Ben & Adam Buening	47
Nicole Bell & Ashley Bell Davis	48
Shabraya & Marjaya	50
Kaitlyn & Alison Hobbs	50
Sarah & Laura	51
Marie & Jennifer Marra	51
Rosalina & Roxana Galaviz	52
Heidi & Kristen	53
Carmen & Camille Thomas	53
Jonta' & Jamison Harris	54
Emma & Kelly Slater	54
Jayde & Charmaine Radford	55
Jordan & Loanne Collyer	55
Karina & Raechelle Banno	56

6 Communicating all day, every day: **57**

7 Long-distance twinning   **61**

Emma Gilmore & Jenny Gilmore Reese	64
Anne Gayson & Trisha Burnett	65
Kayla & Erin	66
Zoe & Rhyan Fingerson	67
Lisa & Ela	67
Jenna & Jane	69

8 Favorite twin moments   **69**

Rachel & Rebekah Aladdin (aka Reine)	71
Divya & Devyani Biswal	72
Sam & Kit Wallen Russell	73
Isaac & Elijah Bell	74

9 Sharing a birthday   **75**

10 Twin humor and pranks   **81**

Adriana & Ariana Sanchez	83
Lindsey McVey & Jenna Elkins	83

Megan & Amanda Morse	84
Gabriella & Graziella Rossetto	84
Tara & Tif Bucknor	85

11 What it is like to work together as twins — 87
Julie Lancia & Jodie Kammerer	90
Armando Soto & Ramón Soto	91
Christelle & Daphné Debauve	92
Dawn & Samantha Goldworm	93
Jordan & Loanne Collyer	93

12 Taking different directions — 95
Allie & Lucie Fink	97
Emma & Kelly Slater	98

13 Arguing — 99
Joyce & Raissa De Haas	101
Ezra & Adeev Potash	102
Eltoria & Nou	102
Emma & Kelly Slater	103
Alexandra & Andrea	104
Charlotte & Heather Howard	104
Rachel & Rebekah Aladdin (aka Reine)	105
Eileen & Gilian Reichert	106
Shanae & Shaniece Cole	106
Alyson & Alayna Thibodeaux	107
Emily & Lyla Allen	107

14 What you should know about twins — 109
Twin parents of Chloe & Lily	111
Cheryl Lage	111
Travis & Lynn Durham	112
Darlene Brisse	113
Coco Goytizolo	113

15 Dating a twin — 115

Lulu & Lala	118
Chad Hatcher	119
Nazar	119
Stuart Chapman	120
Stephen Schlumpf	121

16 Twin parent perspectives — 123

Erica Elizarraraz	125
Mike Davis	126
Twin parents of Chloe & Lily	127
Leah McQueen	128
Greg and Rachel Pinn	129
Thomas Jezequel	129
Courtney El-Ghoul	132
Katelyn Halko	133

17 Advice from twins to other twins — 135

Jennifer & Ashley Rubin	138
Lucy Knott & Kelly Sharpe	139
Jonta' & Jamison Harris	139
Jonathan & Joshua Baker	140
Allie & Lucie Fink	140
Heidi & Kristen	141
Carmen & Camille Thomas	142
Alyson & Alayna Thibodeaux	142

18 Epilogue — 145

Acknowledgements — 147

INDEX — 148

Introduction

It is true, there are more twins today than ever. The twin world is growing. It is also true that twins fascinate people. It may be the twin bond. Born together, best friends forever.

Or maybe it is the fact that it is different from the norm.

Whatever it is, we totally get it. We are twins and we are still fascinated by twins. The twin bond, the twin myths, and the similarities twins seem to have.

From having spent the last two years amassing twin friends around the world, we truly believe that the world needs more knowledge about twins. Twins need to know more about twins. Non-twins need to know what makes twins similar and different.

We also believe everyone can learn from twins. Because, even if we lucked out by being born with our best friend forever (BFF), that doesn't mean that the relationship is perfect. Communication and understanding are key ingredients. And sometimes we have phases where we are more close than others. And even if we have known each other for a whole life-time we learn new things about each other every single day.

That is what is so fascinating about twins to us and why we wanted to learn more.

This book is about the life of twins. It is about the upsides, the downsides, the benefits, the challenges. Advice twins have for non-twins and fellow twins. *The Life of Twins* is essentially about the nitty-gritty of life as a twin.

Chapter one
Who are we and why we are writing this book

You may wonder who are we to write this book? We are K&E, twin sisters and founders of Twinning Store. Growing up, we have always embraced being twins.

As we will discuss in this book, it definitely also has some challenges. But to us, personally, the advantages far outweigh the disadvantages.

A couple of years ago, we were making the same twin joke that we have made a gazillion times before. We were acting out our typical twin dynamic, where K says her bit and E knows where her line fits next. Not being comedians or entertainers, it just occurred to us that we can't be the only twins that do these things.

They say 3% of the world population are twins.[i] If that number is accurate, that means with the world's current population of 7.5 billion the world counts 225 million twins. So although twins are rare, there are still a lot of us. To put in perspective, that is as much as 70% of the US population or more than the entire population of Brazil. And if you count family and friends of twins you can start multiplying how many people are living the twin life.

When we had the epiphany that there must be others out there that like us are looking for questions and answers about twin life, our natural first step was to do a search online to find a twin website. But, we weren't able to find what we were looking for. And so, with our background in fashion and tech, we then decided to take matters into our own hands and started the Twinning Store. Fast forward to today, we have now built a worldwide community of twins and twin parents who follow our blog, stay posted on our social media and rock our twin clothing and accessories.

We still can't believe how much our community has grown. We started our journey not knowing more than a handful of other twins. Now we know thousands and count many of them as our friends. We have their back and they have ours.

From South Africa to Sweden, from toddler age to twins in retirement age, men and women, we all have in common that twin life somehow has affected us.

To us it seems like yesterday that the hashtag #twinfluencer had 5 posts and at the time of writing this the hashtag has been used over 9,000 times and publications such as Vogue Magazine, the Atlantic, Telegraph and Elle have all used the term.

Before we even hit launch, we had decided that we are not the experts of twins. Our relationship may have similarities to other twins, but we are only connoisseurs of our own twin bond. Just as other twins are experts of their relationship. We have therefore since Twinning Store's inception asked other twins for their input. Not knowing a lot of twins, we had to reach out to twins we didn't know. At first it was hard, but over time it has become easier and now we do it on a daily basis.

We love when fellow twins in our community share their point of view and how they sometimes interpret some things differently than us. It adds to our own understanding of our twin bond and we LOVE that. Also, through our blog, we have interviewed twins and twin parents all over the world. And usually there are as many similarities as there are differences. Through us asking questions, and sometimes tough questions, we have been able to learn so much and even gained friends in literally all corners of the world.

When the idea of a book came up, we knew what it had to entail. Being on the receiving end of all the twinsights shared on a daily basis, it only seems fair to share what people have shared with us. In other words, this book isn't just written by us, it is a collective effort from over 120 twins, friends and family. As best possible, we have included twins of all ages and from all continents. In addition, we have made sure to interview a mix of boy/boy twins, girl/girl twins and girl/boy twins to get the most in-depth knowledge base possible. For the same reason, we have tried to represent as many points of view as possible for each topic.

Why read this book?

We are so thankful for you choosing to read this book and want you to know some of the reasons we think you should continue reading.

Historically speaking, twins in many cultures were outcasts, so we are grateful to live in a time and age where that isn't the case. And we love that the popular culture loves twins. We consume any information about twins that we can get our eyes on. But we have sometimes felt that the available information doesn't encapsulate all of what it is like to be a twin. So, this book is our attempt on making the life of twins more attainable for twins and non-twins alike.

Second, we are always trying to use our platform to make it even more meaningful to live the twin life. Through our company, we have gotten countless messages and emails from twins thanking us for shedding light on all sides of being twins (the good and the bad). It is important for us to show that us as twins are same, same, but different. Among us as siblings, but also with other twins. We can learn from each other and that is something we hope this book can show to everyone, twin or not.

Third, this is a book we wish we had growing up. Twins as everyone else goes through phases of ups and downs. Being compared to your best friend when you are trying to find yourself is a unique challenge and we didn't have twins to look up to or ask advice. Our only resource was TV shows and movies and that wasn't always the best reference. It was all trial and error on both our and our parents end, and maybe some things would have been easier if this book was around. We, therefore, hope this book can add as a resource for twins of any age, twin parents, friends or family of twins or someone who is looking for a better insight into twin life. To our best capability we have tried to share insights from all sorts of angles to give you the most extensive and objective information possible. Hopefully we can help clarify some things and even busts some twin stereotypes once and for all.

Lastly, learning from other people about twin life may inspire something in you. All sets of twins are similar but also very different. We can see parallels to that in so many aspects in life. Throughout this book, you will get to know people living the twin life from all over the world. They are represented in different ages, careers, beliefs and genders. In other words, they have similarities and differences just as everyone else. Learning from someone who is seemingly different from you, may help you appreciate something that you had not before. And maybe that can be applied to other aspects of your life as well.

Regardless of why you have chosen to read *The Life of Twins*, we really hope that this book leaves you more knowledgeable about how many amazing twins and stories are out there.

How to read this book

This has been written as a guide and resource to twin life. But nothing stated should be looked at conclusively. As stated, we do not claim to be experts on all things twin. Nor do any of the people we have interviewed. Personally, we have always learned more about ourselves (and our own twin relationship has grown) by asking questions to others. If there is something that occurs as familiar to you that is great. But if something is different from what you are used to then even better and we challenge you to spend time on thinking why it is different.

This book is intended to be read chronologically, so we highly suggest that is how you read it. Once you have read it, we hope that you use it as a resource from time to time. Our hope is that you will also share *The Life of Twins* with anyone that you think could benefit from it.

We are always looking to expand on our twin knowledge and meet more twins, twin parents, or other friends and family of twins. Our large, but tight knit, community has grown online completely organically and by people like you sharing about Twinning Store when you meet other twins. It is crazy to think how far-reaching the community will get if everyone keeps sharing with only one other person. In other words, please don't leave people in the dark - invite them to join our community. The bigger the #twinfluencer family gets, the better for all of us.

We would love if you let us know about your favorite part of this book. Or maybe there is something we can include in future editions. Please email us at book@twinningstore.com or contact us through our website twinningstore.com. And if you have not already, please join us on Instagram @twinning.store.

Xoxo,

K & E

Chapter two
Being called the twins

YOU CAN'T SAY TWIN,
WITHOUT SAYING WIN

TWINNING
store

- **"As a twin I always used to wonder, "Where do I begin, and where does Pati begin? Are she and I the same person, two parts of the same person, or separate entirely?"[ii]**
  - *Gisele Bündchen, model and activist (Twin sister to Patricia Bündchen, manager)*

We can't even remember a time where we weren't referred to as the "twins". The twins that and the twins this. In our early years, it didn't bother us. However, going into the teenage years it sometimes felt like people considered us more a unit than individuals. Luckily later in life, we started embracing it.

For us - it is the ultimate fun fact about ourselves and it has brought us more joy and opportunities than anything else. If anything, we love that our very own VIP club, has a name, "the twins".

As we have already mentioned, our opinion about anything twin related is just our opinion. And we totally understand that to get the best input, we have to ask other twins what they feel about twin life. So, we did a poll of 744 twins where we asked the question "Do you mind being called the twins?" - 75% answered no, and 25% answered yes. The ones that answered that they did mind, said "it makes us seem as one person", whereas the ones that didn't mind said "love being called the twins", "I love it.. knowing that it really means something special to be a twin" and "we are twins, so it makes sense to call us that!".

Twin nicknames

Although we may be called twins by others, we also have nicknames for each other. Our personal favorites for each other are Twin #1 and Twin #2. We also asked on our Instagram what other twins call each other and here are some of our favorite ones:

- Twinny
- Twinny-poo
- Twincess
- Twinsie
- Other half
- Womb Mate
- Gemela
- Sissy
- Twinster
- Evil twin

Twinning fact - DID YOU KNOW?
25% of all identical twins are mirror twins. Mirror twins have features that are opposite of each other, for example, with what way the hair swirls, being left and right-handed, and crossing legs opposite to each other.[iii]

How to say the word twin

We have been fortunate to be able to travel to many great places in the world, either for awesome twincations or for work. One of the first things we always try to learn is how to say the word *twin* or *twins*. It is a great way to get to know the language, but also to form new friendships. Once someone hears we are twins, almost always, someone knows another set of twins.

One time, a taxi driver in Italy, had twin daughters the same age as us, and we swapped so many notes and it even inspired some of our most popular Instagram memes (side note: we unfortunately didn't get his information, so we do hope that this book somehow gets in his hands).

Twinput

Being that the #twinfluencer community is global, we of course, had to ask the community how they say the word twin in their language. We wish we could share all of the responses, but here is 15 different ways:

1. Marina & Sabrina (@marina_sabrina), France - French:
    - Jumeaux (when two boys are twins or one girl and one boy are twins) and jumelles (when two girls are twins)

2. Isidora & Antonia Hernández-Rudnick (@isidorah98 and @anto_h) Viña del Mar, Chile - Spanish:
    - Gemela (when two girls are twins) and gemelo (when two boys are twins)

3. Leni & Lotta (@laurilovesnework) Cologne, Germany - German:
    - Zwilling

4. Angelica Bula (@lika_86x_), Chicago, USA - Polish:
   - Bliźnięta

5. Rhonda Gibbons (@gibbons_rhonda) San Diego, USA - English:
   - Twin

6. Ane Ludwig (@ane.27), Basque Country - Basque language:
   - Bikiak

7. Halla Maria Þorsteinsdóttir (@hallamaria1), Reykjavík, Iceland - Icelandic:
   - Tvíburi

8. Linette and Henriette Laumann (@linettelaumann), Denmark - Danish:
   - Tvilling

9. Eva & Julia Schnabl (@evaschnabl and @julia_schnabl), Styria, Austria - German:
   - Zwilling

10. Meghan (@findingmegsiemoo), Cape Town, South Africa:
    - It's tweeling in Afrikaans, twin in English and amawele in Xhosa

11. Sara & Lobke Verboom (@saraverboom and @lobkeverboom), Netherlands - Dutch:
    - Tweeling

12. Maram & Mayssoune (@maroandmaysotwins), Egypt - Arabic:
    - توأم (Taw2am)

13. Idhikaa & Ishikaa Rekhi (@rekhiidhaa), New Delhi, India - Hindi:
    - Judwaa

14. Natalia & Vanessa Bartolenová (@nati_muc and @vanessa_muc_), Slovakia - Slovak:
    - Dvojičky

15. Adrian & Adriana Cruze (@thecruzetwins), Colombo, Sri Lanka - Sinhalese:
    - Nivuun daruwo/ nivun-no

Twinning fact - DID YOU KNOW?

The word twin is probably derived from an ancient German word twine,
which means 'two together.[iv]

Did you learn a new way to say twin? When we asked on our Instagram "Do you know how to say twin in more than one language?", 76% said yes. How awesome is that? We really encourage you to figure out as many ways to say it. It is fun and as mentioned it has brought us so many awesome experiences. In the next chapter, we will explore some of the other fun sides of being twins.

Chapter three
Perks of being twins

I GOT 99 PROBLEMS
BUT BEING A TWIN AIN'T ONE

TWINNING
store

- **"We do everything together... It's like a marriage and a partnership. We have had ups and downs. It's been 32 years of learning how to communicate. We came out of the womb doing that.**[v]**"**
    - *Mary-Kate and Ashley Olsen, fashion designers and actresses*

It goes without saying, but there are countless perks of being twins. From being born together to sharing important moments in life together. Being a twin is the best! If you are a twin, then you probably have your own list of why it is cool. But that list can always be expanded, so this chapter will explore some of the twin perks.

One of our favorite things about being twins is that we always have each other and the feeling of comfort that brings. We have literally never had to look for a best friend, as we came into the world with ours. They say that best friends can sit next to each other and not talk but still feel social. That is how we have had it our entire life. We sometimes joke that we are twintroverted. Not extroverted or introverted, but twintroverted. Meaning we have it easiest when we are around each other.

It's not like we can't hang out with others, we both have friends and relationships independent of each other. But when we are together, we recharge like we would with alone time. We don't have to talk or be afraid of taking up too much space, because we are so in sync. And so honest! We know that if one of us has issues with something, we will not sugar coat it and just say it right out. Friends and family might be surprised by our brutal honesty, but we don't even think about it.

Another favorite perk about being twins is twincations! If you are not familiar with the term, twincation is a vacation that twins take together. Some twins take them solo, and some take them with other friends and family. We have done both. Our absolute favorite is to go somewhere beautiful.

Luckily, we live in Los Angeles, which is located close to so many amazing places and so twincations can be as little as half an hour away. We can drive up Pacific Coast Highway with our Kindles filled with reading material, a picnic bag and just hang out. When we have more time on our hands, we will jet off in a plane somewhere in the world and rent a car and go on a road trip. When we get hungry, which is usually at the same time, we will both be in unison about what to eat. On all twincations we end up with some great memories as we are equally adventurous and always in sync about what to do.

Twinput

This feeling of comfort, sharing adventures and being completely familiar with each other's interests - is one of the best things about being twins. There are many, many more perks, so we had to ask some fellow twins what they love about being twins:

Hannah & Jess Gerlacher

Location: Dallas, TX, United States
Occupation: College students

Also known as the SOT twins, we are twenty years old and identical twins. We live together and spend the majority of our free time together and are super close!

- "It is a bond like no other."

Lucy Knott & Kelly Sharpe

Location: Stockport, United Kingdom
Occupation: Teaching Assistants, Bloggers & Authors.

We are former professional wrestlers who love all things Italy, food and books. When not working with children we adore writing; Lucy writes romance novels, Kelly writes children's books. We love spending time with family and each other and being twins is one of our favorite things!

- "Having a built-in best friend has allowed us to be confident when stepping out of our comfort zones, as you know you've always got someone by your side that's got your back. Plus, it's a great ice breaker when meeting new people."

Megan & Liz

Location: Nashville, TN, United States
Occupation: Musician, Influencers and Boutique Owners

We are absolutely those twins who work together and love every second of it. We are so lucky that our passions are lined up for us to be able to both do what we love, with each other. We make the perfect team because we both have different strengths. Either way, we are very thankful for each other.

- "It's the most special bond that still to this day is impossible for us to put into words. It's literally unexplainable and magic."

Bud & Aidan Brenna Williams

Location: London, United Kingdom
Occupation: Actors, models and musicians

We are currently playing in our punk and hip-hop band We Are One. We have been writing music together and playing in bands since the age of 13 and have played shows all over the UK.

- "A HUGE strength not only have we always had someone to have our back, we also have always split everything in half, such as workload or costs…"

Lisa Marie Elwes & Janet Kurbikoff

Location: Malibu, CA, United States
Occupation: Stills photographer & proud stay-at-home mother and interior designer & actress on the side

- Lisa Marie: "When I came out, they weighed me and started wrapping me up when suddenly the doctor shouted, "WAIT, THERE'S ANOTHER ONE!" 7 minutes later, my tiny twin sister was born. Some say our hearts must have been beating at the same time and I'm certain they still do! She is my womb-mate, my soulmate, my everything."

Chloé & Francesca Townsend

Location: Essex, United Kingdom
Occupation: Fitness Instructors

27-year-old twins from Essex, we love everything about being Twins, we always dress the same for our work and now when we go out together! Twinning is Winning!

- "Being twins is really special, obviously we don't know any different, but being a twin is great as you are never alone and there's always someone to share experiences with, it's fun accomplishing things together!"

Eric Niyomwungere & Aimable Niyongabo

Location: Salt Lake City, UT, United States
Occupation: Recording Artist

We were born in Tanzania, Africa, in 1997 and then our family migrated to the US in 2007. During my high school days, we pursued music and we have released numerous songs/videos on YouTube and other musical platforms under the name Young Spit.

- "No matter what happens, I have my twin brother whom I can always count on or go to."

Twinning fact - DID YOU KNOW?
Although polar bears can give birth to one to three cubs, they most commonly give birth to twins (mostly fraternal but sometimes identical too)[vi]

Kevin & Chris Delgado

Location: Leamington, Ontario, Canada
Occupation: DJs and Producer

The identical twin brothers form the DJ duo, "TWINNS". The name TWINNS just sort of felt perfect as growing up we were called twins. So we figured to find a way to make it sort of original by adding the double "N" to signify the two of us.

- "It is technically like being born with an unplanned best friend. It's AWESOME!"

Charlotte & Heather Howard

Location: Bedfordshire, United Kingdom and Perth, Australia
Occupation: International Operations Coordinator and Event Coordinator

We both love to travel and to try new things. We love to have a drink and share the same sense of humour in whatever we do! We are extremely close, argue a lot but always make up within minutes

- "Looking at each other and knowing exactly what's she's thinking just by her expression. No-one else understands!"

Julia and Michael Toronczak

Location: San Diego, CA, United States
Occupation: Student

K&E: That the twin bond is special is widely known, but that doesn't stop us from being amazed by it over and over again. A set of twins that continue to move us is the twins behind the blog, Beyond the Waves, Julia and Michael Toronczak. Their bond and story is truly unique. We are so twinspired by the important awareness work they are doing, so we asked Julia to tell their story in their words:

My name is Julia Toronczak and I'm beyond grateful for my twin brother, Michael. He may not speak to me in words, but he communicates through love better than anyone I know. My twin has Down syndrome, and is such a loving light. Even without words, we still have a "telepathic" understanding of what's going on with each other. In our population, twins account for approximately 3% of births. That percentage drops even more in the case of Down Syndrome, where one twin is affected, and the other is not. And I couldn't imagine a better twin to have.

Growing up with Michael has taught me the importance of unconditionally loving yourself and all the lives you encounter. And having him as a twin has made it even better. We've been together since before day 1. We both entered the world as each other's best friends, and that bond is infinite. We've grown up with an inseparable connection that's unique. Having a sibling with special needs is already rewarding, but even more so when they are your twin. I love my little dude who's also my best friend!

Albert & Robert Gomez

Location: Canyon Country, CA, United States

- "We share friends, so we all hang out."

Alexis & Samantha Belbel

Location: Dallas, TX, United States
Occupation: Bloggers and owners of Adoubledose.com

We are besties with a love for fashion and healthy living. We have always been interested in anything related to beauty, wellness, and travel, so we enjoy sharing those topics with our audience! Our favorite thing is connecting with people all over the world!

- "It's an amazing bond that you can't describe. It's literally your other half."

We feel so lucky to have been born twins. There are so many perks and the community keep reminding of us more every day. Being a twin is unique and as we like to say "the twin bond is stronger than James Bond". However, being twins is not always just sunshine, which we will explore in the next chapter.

Chapter four
Downsides to being twins

WHEN PEOPLE START
POINTING OUT ALL THE DIFFERENCES
BETWEEN YOU AND YOUR TWIN

TWINNING
store

- "My sister and I used to read every fan mail because we just love our fans that much. And we used to sign the autographs... It wasn't pre-made. So I can remember reading this stupid letter when this person called me ugly and said I was the 'ugly and goofy twin.' And for years, I made an agreement with that stupid statement. And I carried it around with me for years. I thought I was ugly and I thought I was goofy. My amazing best friend said, 'You know what Tamera? You are not 16 years old anymore. You do not need to listen to that insecurity in your head anymore. You do not let other people define who you are."[vii]

- *Tamera Mowry-Housley, actress (Twin sister to Tia Mowry-Hardrict, actress)*

Being a twin is an amazing journey. It is (as we have covered) a life filled with perks from the time we are born. Sometimes it feels that most people think that the twin life is free of arguments and problems. However, being twins, can at times be very challenging. In this chapter, we will explore some of the downsides to the twin life.

One aspect that comes to mind, is how there has always been constant comparison. We were told by teachers growing up if we weren't performing at the same pace or if we did something different from each other. As we will explore further in later in this chapter, people will sometimes say cruel things and when we were young it was harder to deal with.

Not doing well on a test is not fun on it's own, but having a teacher say "why did you not do as well as your twin?" was even worse.

Luckily for us, the constant comparison and comments eventually turned into healthy competition that has helped us succeed in many areas of our lives. Because, we always knew that if one of us was able to do it, like for example cooking or playing sports, the likelihood of both being able was much higher, especially with practice. Sure it was sometimes an uphill battle, but knowing that someone so close to us had accomplished it felt like the push we needed. This healthy competition has made us work harder and has in most cases only been a positive.

Another challenging aspect is that when we were in our teens and people started going to house parties, it was more than once we didn't get invited. How we interpreted that was that we weren't cool enough or that people didn't want to hang out with us. However, when we brought it up to the people who held the parties, it couldn't be more far from the truth.

In their mind, the two of us had our own thing going on and didn't appear to have time for anything else. With that out the way, we started getting invited and everyone was happy. It was a powerful lesson for us and something that we have thought of often later in life. Luckily, it made our twin bond stronger and eventually even more proud to be twins.

Although, that specific situation solved itself, it is something we have seen time and time again. People tend to group twins together. We do it too. Because it is hard not to do it. In the same way, it is sometimes hard to separate band players from the entire band.

One of the most gratifying parts of Twinning Store for us is to shed light on some of these twin specific challenges, because we were never able to ask other twins about these things growing up. And more than once have we been moved to tears by some of the messages we have received from twins and twin parents.

One might share how a blog post we have written gave them a different perspective or that reading someone's Instagram comment has helped them not feel alone. And for us personally, getting to know other twins have really helped us get to know our twinship better and have a better understanding of why certain things are like they are.

Twinput

In trying to learn more about some of the not so pleasant sides of being twins, we consulted some #twinfluencers about their experiences:

Jennifer & Ashley Rubin

Location: San Francisco, CA, United States
Occupation: Owners of Native Twins Coffee & Native Twins Granola

Jen and Ash are identical mirror image twins from Mill Valley, Ca. Best friends & business partners. Jen was born 7 minutes first, she's a lefty and a tomboy at heart, leader of the pack, she's always got her game face on. Ashley is right-handed and a girly girl at heart, she's the bubbly one, always smiling and laughing. They balance each other out and make a great team as the dynamic duo!

- "A major weakness is that it can be tricky for others and even ourselves to recognize our individuality & independence because we are so close & often dependent on one another."

Destiny Mitchell & Alexxus Mitchell

Location: Tampa, FL, United States
Occupation: Retail Associates & College Students

We are both fraternal twins but look identical. We are currently studying at Pasco Hernando Community State College - Destiny is majoring in Speech Pathology and Alexxus is majoring in Physical Therapy. We both work part time jobs at the same mall, but at different retail stores. During our free time we love to dance.

- "When someone says one twin looks better than the other, or when people count you as one person."

Rachel & Rebekah Aladdin (aka Reine)

Location: Los Angeles, CA, United States
Occupation: Director of Executive Recruiting and Celebrity Make-up Artist

The Aladdin twins, Rebekah and Rachel, are multi-talented twin sisters based out of LA. While Rebekah is a celebrity make-up artist and Rachel, has made a solid career for herself in a completely different industry as a Director of Executive Recruiting. Outside of their everyday careers, they both sing and model.

- "Being a twin is as awesome as it sounds, but it's also a lot of work! You have a whole other person that you are responsible for and your level of responsibility and commitment to each other constantly changes as you grow through life. It's weird to come into the world with someone, grow up together, have very similar life experiences, and then wake up one day and realize you are two very different people. It's a relationship that's constantly growing and changing. People assume that twins HAVE to be close, but they don't. It's a decision that we make and constantly work towards."

Milena & Jelena Aleksic

Location: United States
Current occupation: Influencers

We are bloggers and influencers who believe in the magic of this life and do our best to convey that through photography. Jelena is a certified Acrovinyasa yoga teacher and has a BS degree in Sports Science and Physical education. Milena is also a yogi, a mom to beautiful baby Selena and a Med school student. We are both founders of our own activewear brand.

- "Back in the days when we were in elementary school and high school, everyone bullied us for being identical. The kids were cruel and didn't like anyone standing out from the rest. They called us "special" but not in a good way and made us feel like weirdos. It was a difficult period for us, but the good thing was that we weren't alone. We had each other and going through hell only made our bond even stronger. We knew that what we had was a unique privilege and that's what helped us survive through school. Probably the most important thing would be that, even though we look almost identical, we are not the same person! We have been treated like we are one person, not two separate individuals, more than a handful of times. It's a terrible and degrading thing, to say the least. We agree on a lot of things, but we are also very different from each other and people should understand that. For example, Milena is more shy and introvert and Jelena is more friendly and extrovert. Milena is a genius for math and sciences, while Jelena is terrible at those. Jelena likes horror movies, while Milena hates them. See what we're talking about?"

Annette Schreyer & Birgitte Schreyer Duarte

Location: Rome, Italy and Toronto, Canada
Occupation: Jewelry Designer and Theatre Director & Translator

Annette and Birgitte grew up in Munich, where they both studies theatre studies. A research scholarship led Birgitte to try out life in Toronto, Canada, where she now works as a freelance director, dramaturg and translator in Toronto, where she lives with her husband and her young daughter. Anette now live mostly in Rome, Italy, where she is a photographer, jewelry designer, singer of baroque music and a cancer survivor. Two years ago, she was diagnosed with breast cancer - exactly the time when her twin was pregnant with her little daughter. Now that she has overcome the illness, she able to enjoy her little niece, who seems to be their "third twin"!

- "As kids, we didn't enjoy all aspects of twinhood, even though we always loved being together non-stop. We didn't like being compared at all stages of growing up; we thought people should make more of an effort to tell us apart, and we were very focused on each other as pre-schoolers and didn't make friends easily at first. But none of that really mattered in contrast to the special connection we always felt with each other."

Carmen & Camille Thomas

Occupation: Musicians
Location: Los Angeles, CA, United States

We are Canadian twins living in LA who write and play music together. Camille plays guitar, Carmen plays flute and we love harmonizing. We believe in spreading love and kindness through who we are as people and through our music.

- "It can be a bit of a crutch sometimes as we always have each other so we don't need a lot of outside friendships but we are trying to expand our bubble."

Everyone faces challenges in life, and twins are no different. It is easy to think that twin life is perfect as it may look like that from the outside.

We hope that hearing about other twins having had challenges can be helpful and educational. It has been for us. Now, let us move on to the many twin questions people ask.

Chapter five
Common twin questions

IDENTICAL OR FRATERNAL?

TWINNING
store

- **"We've been asked a lot about where we met and I say "the womb". They look at us funny... and I'm like, 'No, we really did meet in the womb, we're twins."**[viii]

- Jessica Origliasso, singer, The Veronicas (Twin sister to Lisa Origliasso, singer, The Veronicas)

People find twins fascinating and you early on get used to expect the twin questions. Honestly, we can't remember a time someone didn't ask us about twin life. Before starting Twinning Store, we didn't have the full appreciation for why. But after starting our company, we hear ourselves asking twins twin questions regularly. We even asked tons of them when writing this book. And if you've been one of the people asking these questions, don't worry. Unless we are having a bad day and not up for a conversation, we honestly enjoy answering them. And if anything, we are excited to answer any questions you may have. Who doesn't want to talk about their best friend?

When we were born, there were no identical or fraternal tests taken and therefore we don't know if we are fraternal or identical. This is not as uncommon as you think, as many fellow twins have shared that it is the same for them. But, when we get the question all twins (and twin parents) get: "Identical or fraternal?" - that question always starts a discussion. It usually goes something like this:

- "Are you identical or fraternal?"
- Us: We don't know
- "Wait, can you stand next to each other?"
- Us: Yeah, ok
- "I think you are identical" or "I think you are fraternal"

Same procedure every time. There were times in our teenage years when this standing next to each other and being compared was the absolute worst. But now we just enjoy the moment and accept it for what it is. Why not? Often, it is the best conversation opener and we have often gotten to know people quicker that way. It is rare people ask a question we haven't heard before and so to people's amusement we often give our answers at the same time.

Twinput

We asked our fellow twins about what typical questions they are used to hearing and here is what they have to say:

Stephanie Dickinson

Location: Central Coast, NSW, Australia
Occupation: Primary School Teacher

My name is Steph and I have a twin brother. I love my job and I absolutely love going to the beach with family and friends.

- "People always ask if we are alike and if we are close."

David & Fidel Solorzano

Location: Orange County, CA, United States
Occupation: David is in Property Management and Fidel is a Veterinary Technician

We were born in raised in Orange County, California and spent summers on our parents ranch outside Eugene, Oregon. We initially pursued careers in the Veterinary field, working together at general practice for 5 years... often confusing clients.

- "If I hit you will he feel it? Or have you ever traded places?"

Jessica & Stephanie

Location: Toronto, ON, Canada
Occupation: Jessica is an educational Assistant for kids with special needs. Stephanie doesn't work because she has special needs. She spends her days living her best life at her day program for young adults with special needs! :)

, a twin is the coolest experience! The one thing that ninds me that I'm a twin is my career. I do what I do ie influence of my twin who has special needs. I wou.~ who I am without her, and I'm forever grateful for her. Stephanie is the happiest person you'll ever meet. She always has the biggest smile on her face and it's truly infectious! She is non verbal, and so when it comes to explaining our "twin" story, she loves to always hear me say "Stephanie was born first".

"Some questions we often got before are:

- do you know what each other are thinking?
- are you guys identical or fraternal?
- who was born first?
- how many minutes apart are you guys?
- Or sometimes when having a twin comes out in a conversation, we usually get "YOU'RE A TWIN?!" And then have to go through the wholeeeeee series of questions just listed and more!"

Ben & Adam Buening

Location: Saint Henry, Ohio
Occupations: Ministry Director and Elementary School Teacher

We grew up in the best neighborhood of four houses in which 3 of the 4 houses had a set of male twins… we believe there was something in the water! The only house that didn't have a set of male twins had all girls! In our opinion, "twin life" is the best life.

- Do you like being a twin?

- What is it like being a twin? (Don't know...never been not a twin LOL)
- Do you have twin telepathy?
- Can you feel what your twin is feeling?
- How can you tell each other apart?
- Do you have the same friends?
- Are you identical? (Most people think my twin and I are even though we are not.)
- What's the longest you've ever been apart?
- Do you miss your twin?

Nicole Bell & Ashley Bell Davis

Location: Broussard, LA and Youngsville, LA, United States
Occupation: Photographer at Nicole Bell Photography, LLC and Construction Project Manager at Davis Design & Consulting, LLC

We are both self-employed and creatives who love to travel and spend lots of time with family. We were born 20 minutes apart and are polar opposites in almost every way. Even our blood types are opposite. Although we don't look alike, people somehow still get our names mixed up.

- "People ask if we are identical (we look nothing alike) so clearly they have no clue what the difference is"

Twinning fact - DID YOU KNOW?
The West African country of Benin has the highest national average of twinning, with a rate of 27.9 twins per 1,000 births"[ix]

The not so cool twin questions

Some questions are not as nice. People can say interesting things and especially when we were younger and not prepared it could be especially hurtful. These are the moments having twin role models would have been great. Even just knowing through the Twinning Store community that other twins have been through the same, has made us stronger and more capable to handle certain things. There is something in knowing that when it happens to others too that is isn't about us personally.

To this date, the worst for us is when someone says something like "Do you know you are my favorite twin?". Maybe the person can't see the harm in it and is just trying to be nice, but it is essentially an insult towards our oldest and bestest friend. And the fact that we can't say that to the one person we care the most about, makes it even worse.

Comments and questions on the way we look can be hurtful too. But now as adults, we have the experience, know who we are and have some awesome clap backs. Like one time when someone said that K was prettier than E, E clapped back saying: "Wow, what a nice thing to say?" and the person felt embarrassed and apologized.

Twinput

Curious what experiences other twins have had, we asked some twinfluencers "Are there any questions that annoy or hurt you?":

Shabraya & Marjaya

Location: Tucson, AZ, United States
Occupation: Case Administrator and Labor and Delivery Scrub Tech

We're opposites in some areas, the same in most others. Shay is the leader and more independent. Jay is more quiet and can be more dependent, but keeps Shay grounded and "humble" but trolling her on Instagram. We both have good hearts and at the end of the day want the same thing - just might go about getting it differently.

- "Which one is the mean one, which one is the nice one?"

Kaitlyn & Alison Hobbs

Location: Fullerton, CA, United States
Occupation: Dance Majors in College

We are fraternal twins, but we look identical. People think we are lying when we tell them otherwise. We are sophomores in college and are studying dance. We have a close bond with each other because we moved from state to state, so we could be considered as best friends!

- "I never really get annoyed when people ask the same questions about being a twin. I do get annoyed when people only address us as "the twins." Like, I am my own person and would like to be treated as an individual sometimes, if you know what I mean, haha. The one question that does hurt me a little when people ask me is "Who do you think is prettier out of the two of you?". Every person is pretty in their own ways, and we look the same so, we are both pretty."

Sarah & Laura

Location: Ontario, Canada
Occupation: Self-employed

We are fraternal twins, but we look identical. People think we are lying when we tell them otherwise. We are sophomores in college and are studying dance. We have a close bond with each other because we moved from state to state, so we could be considered as best friends!

- "We look nothing alike, like nothing alike. So, one question is that we have gotten that annoys me is when we said "we are twins" and some people said no, you can't be twins or when they kind of look at us funny because we don't look alike"

Marie & Jennifer Marra

Location: Boston, MA, United States

Occupation: Director of the Lobbying Division of the Secretary of the Commonwealth's office and Legislative Secretary for the Secretary of the Commonwealth's office.

We both love being twins and are the best of friends. We both love shopping, traveling and going on different twin adventures.

- "Yes. Someone in middle school asked why I was so ugly but my twin was so cute? And thought we were lying because we don't look alike."

We assume that the many twin questions stem from myths about twins. Myths of which there are many. This is normal with something so fascinating and unique as twins. Some things may be true for some twins and not for others.

Twinput

We asked some #twinfluencers what misconceptions they think people have about twins:

Rosalina & Roxana Galaviz

Location: Los Angeles, CA, United States
Occupation: Influencers

Also known as R al Cuadro, we are twins sharing our passion: Fashion, to inspire others to try something different

- "That twins can read and communicate with their minds."

Heidi & Kristen

Location: Minneapolis, MN, United States
Occupation: RN Care Coordinator and Lease Closing Specialist

We grew up in Wisconsin, went to college in different states and then both ended up in Minneapolis, MN. We've always taken our own paths, but have found a way to be involved in each other's lives. Heidi has a Wheaten Terrier and works as an RN Care Coordinator and Kristen has a Beagle mix, works as a Lease Closing Specialist and lives with her husband and new baby girl.

- "That we can read each other's minds and feel each other's pain; also that twins never disagree or argue. We also think the biggest misconception people have is that twins are the same. We are similar in some ways but we actually have a lot of differences! Another misconception is that we can read each other's minds."

Carmen & Camille Thomas

Location: Los Angeles, CA, United States
Occupation: Musicians

We are Canadian twins living in LA who write and play music together. Camille plays guitar, Carmen plays flute and we love harmonizing. We believe in spreading love and kindness through who we are as people and through our music.

- "That we would ever date the same guy. It's sad how many times that question gets asked."

Jonta' & Jamison Harris

Location: Los Angeles, CA, United States
Occupation: Digital Marketing and Fashion Experts

With their amazing style and fashion sense, Jonta and Jamison Harris, aka the Harris twins, have built up a worldwide following of people carefully paying attention to the twin brothers' moves. In addition, the twin brothers are digital media experts and have a website filled with great advice and tips.

- "We think the biggest misconception about twins is that we are the same person. Yes, we share the same face, and lots of similarities, but we are still individuals at the end of the day."

Emma & Kelly Slater

Emma and Kelly Slater
Location: Los Angeles, CA, United States
Occupation: Dancing with the Stars Professional Dancer and Seamstress

The Slater sisters grew up in Tamworth, UK. They attended school together and though their careers lead them through different forms of education after high school, they now both live happily in Los Angeles.

- "Just don't treat twins the same just because they're twins. And definitely don't be mean to one twin unless you'll wanna make two enemies."

Jayde & Charmaine Radford

Location: Central Coast, Australia
Occupation: We both work at our father's pool shop "Paramount Pool Centre Sydney 2112"
Jayde is the manager and Charmaine is in retail sales.

We are twins. Ying and yang - we complement each other. An introvert and an extrovert. Fearless and cautious - we always bring the other one out of each other's comfort zones. Together we are the ultimate twin team.

- "Just because fraternal twins don't look like identical twins do, doesn't mean we don't connect and feel each other's pain, or happiness. Whether you have a twin brother or sister twins ultimately share such an unbelievable bond, and it's such an amazing and beautiful feeling!"

Jordan & Loanne Collyer

Location: London, United Kingdom
Occupation: Digital influencers & DJs

We're Jordan and Loanne, identical twin sisters who have grown up by the sea in Portugal with similar interests in travelling, fashion, music and food! We're not only twins but business partners and best friends (worst enemies at times too) but that's only normal!

- "Everyone should know that even though we have a very strong bond, a great connection, we are individual people too!"

Karina & Raechelle Banno

Location: Sydney, Australia
Occupation: Actors and film-makers

Karina has worked both in front and behind the camera in projects such as The Letdown, Mr. Inbetween & Friday on My Mind. Raechelle, an actor and writer, is probably best known for her role as Olivia in the Australian hit show Home and Away (the show chronicles the lives, loves, happiness and heart-breaks of the residents of Summer Bay, a small coastal town in New South Wales, Australia).

- Karinna: "That we have full telepathic conversations. Not so much. But there is something unspoken and understood within a 'look'. We also tend to start sentences and just know where it's going so we don't continue (much to the confusion/annoyance of those around us)."

In general, we love when people ask us about twin life. We embrace it and really recommend doing that as the questions won't disappear. Being a twin is unique and people are curious what it is like. As we mentioned in the beginning of this chapter, we find ourselves asking the standard twin questions all the time. So we get it.

Some things people say on the other hand, like hurtful questions and comments, are not fair. But as with a lot of things in life, it is just something one can't avoid. The best advice we have for fellow twins is to try to your best ability to get used to the questions and comments. Maybe even think ahead on how you would respond if you got one of the questions mentioned above? Our hope is that by educating people, for example with this book, on what is acceptable to say and what is not these incidents will happen less over time. Now, let's talk twin myths.

Chapter six
Communicating all day, every day

TEXTING

WITH EVERYBODY ELSE

WITH MY TWIN

TWINNING store

"[They] talk to each other all the time, and like all children they sometimes can be a little abrupt, a little hard even in their exchanges, but they support each other unconditionally."[x]

- *Princess Charlene of Monaco about her twins Prince Jacques and Princess Gabriella*

We communicate ALL day long - 24/7 and doesn't matter if we are in different continents and time zones. Maybe we got used to constantly communicating already in the womb and we have just continued it once out in the real world - who knows?

When we hang out, we will be talking non-stop and often people around us will roll their eyes at our half sentences and how we cut each other off. We wouldn't dare communicating the same way with others, because it would seem rude and abrupt. But to us, it is our natural way of communicating. And why take time to explain something when we already know what each other is thinking about? Like when K knows what E means when she says "you know that woman at the bus" (although the mentioned lady at the bus is from over 10 years ago).

If we are not in the office or hanging out, we will constantly be texting or FaceTiming. True story: When E deleted our chain of text messages, she freed up 40% space on her phone. All the screenshots, photos and videos we share throughout a day adds up. We also always try to keep each other posted on where we are. So it is not rare that before going into movies E texts K "About to watch XYZ and therefore unable to text for the next two hours" and then text immediately after "Back and ready to text".

To us, it has always been that way but technology has also made it easier. The funny part to our parents is the amount of different ways we communicate and that we can never get enough.

We polled 386 twins and 90% of the ones polled said they talk to their twin every day. We then asked the #twinfluencer community "In what ways have you communicated with your twin today?" and these are some of the responses:

- Iris Oliveira Lima & Jessica Oliveira Lima (@irisolli and @1jessolli), Três Corações, MG, Brazil:
    - "In person, WhatsApp, Instagram, Twitter, text, email, phone calls and telepathically."
- Melissa & Jill Moree (@melissamoree & @jillmoree), Vancouver, BC, Canada:
    - "In person, many texts, and Instagram messages"
- Natalia Calderón Arreola & Isabella Calderón Arreola (@twinsnatisa), Tijuana, México:
    - "In person"
- Becca & Leah Edwards (@beckvand & @limeleahcroix), Baltimore, MD, United States:

- "Text, snap, Instagram and I usually call her on my way home from work"
- Alexandra & Ashton neurauter(@blondie2539), Vancouver Island, BC, Canada:
    - "Text, Instagram, Facebook, and Facetime!"
- Tanya & Felecia Feketitsch (@teatime3 and @lilfekk), Chicago, IL, United States
    - "The best is when we Facetime.. Black screens, just talking, doing stuff on our phones and sending each other pictures and talking about them"

Twinning fact - DID YOU KNOW?

It has been found in a study done in 2011 by researchers at Umberto Castiello of the University of Padova in Italy that twins form a way to communicate already in the womb. The researchers said that their studies revealed that the twins made distinct gestures toward each other.[xi]

Twins communicate a lot and in many different ways. We have always said that there should be free calls and texting between twins, but we have had no luck with that so far. But what do you do if you and your twin are in different places? Doing long-distance twinning if you would like. We will learn more about that next.

Chapter seven
Long-distance twinning

NOTHING CAN COME BETWIN US

TWINNING
store

"The best birthday present I ever got was 10 minutes after I was born."

- Tom Kaulitz, guitarist, Tokio Hotel (and twin brother to Bill Kaulitz, lead singer, Tokio Hotel

Since starting Twinning Store, one of the most frequently asked questions we get from twins is how to maintain the twin bond while being in separate places. The question is usually posed before moving to different cities because of studies or work. Of course, there is a lot of emotions and nerves involved.

We still remember going to different colleges and how exciting and nerve-wracking it was at the same time. Being in a long-distance relationship with your twin can be difficult. As twins you are used to hanging out non-stop from early on so being separated is an adjustment.

We live in the same city now, but we have had stints where we lived on different coasts and even different continents. In other words, we know how hard it can be to be separated from your twin. Going to different colleges, moving with work, or just traveling can be busy and chaotic and may even put a strain on the twin bond. However, we also know from experience, that with some work and communication on both ends it can both work and sometimes even improve your twin relationship. And thankfully, with all the amazing technology available out there, there's no reason to let distance stop hangouts.

These are our top three advice from when we were doing long-distance:

1. Watch the same TV show at the same time

We actually do a count-down to make sure we're reacting to the funny jokes and the tear-jerkers at the same time.

2. Work out together

YouTube is filled with great work-out videos. Find one and play on your computer and use your phone to video chat with your twin. This is a great way to stay in shape too.

3. Plan a trip together

Not being able to spend time with your twin can be tough, but having a future plan for the next time to see each other can make it a little bit easier. Maybe plan to meet half-way, or in the home-town of one of you?

Twinput

We asked the #twinfluencer community on advice on how they best handle living in different places. This is what these twins who are currently long-distance twinning had to share:

Emma Gilmore & Jenny Gilmore Reese

Locations: Dublin, Ireland and Virginia, United States
Occupations: Police Officer and Director of Admission at Health Facility

We have the best time whenever we are together, although it is a rare occasion nowadays we make the most of it! I think the distance has actually made us closer. Jenny has always been the considerate twin where as I would be a bit less serious at times! Jenny is my best friend and I can't wait until we can hang out again and wear our matching t-shirts.

- "We speak almost every day either by text or over the phone, the 5 hour time difference is easy for us now but was hard at the start. We still call each other at the same time on occasion! We still finish each other's sentences and know what the other is going to say next"

Anne Gayson & Trisha Burnett

Location: United Kingdom and Ireland
Occupation: Dance Majors in College

It's a unique bond that is totally unexplained. We are both 54. But we really feel as if we are in our twenties still. Our children love us the fun we have together. We probably drive everyone mad. A language all of its own.

- "We have lived apart for on recent times just 1 year. However we did live apart for almost 10 years before. We speak via Web chat at least 5 times a week for at least an hour or more. If not twice a day. It's so natural to communicate on a daily basis. We just love chatting and having fun. Laughing. Video chat is always best. You can cook together. Really is like being in the same room."

Twinning fact - DID YOU KNOW?
Using an ultrasound isn't the only way doctors can detect a twin pregnancy — some figure it out when they hear two tiny heartbeats through their stethoscope.[xii]

Kayla & Erin

Location: Philadelphia, PA & Los Angeles, CA, United States
Occupation: Librarian & Archivist and Design Manager

We grew up in Northern New Jersey and had always been very close. As babies we even had our own language and name for each other. We attended the same college, but then post-college Erin got a job offer 3,000 miles away. This was the first time we had ever been apart. It's been 7 years since she moved across the country and it has luckily brought us closer.

- "I live in Pennsylvania outside Philly and she lives in Los Angeles (about 3000 miles away). We see each other twice a year for Christmas and a summer trip where she flies back East and I also try and fly out there once a year but haven't had the chance to in a few years. My advice to other twins would be to check in often. Text, phone calls, and especially FaceTime are your friends. Also make an effort to communicate in-depth often and not just surface stuff. Dive in deep about what's going on in each other's lives to keep your connection strong since physically you can't be together. Also try not to let the distance get to you. Absence truly makes the heart grow fonder. My twin and I have become far more closer since she moved across the country than we were living in the same area."

Zoe & Rhyan Fingerson

Location: West Palm Beach, Fl and Warrenton, MI, United States
Occupation: Student and Intern

Rhyan is the quieter twin, but when you get to know her she's wild. She loves to play ukulele and guitar and loves anything Disney. She is studying Children's Ministry at PBA. Zoe is the older twin, and she is full of love and light. Her energy is contagious, and she always has something funny to say. She has a deep appreciation for music and loves to play guitar.

- "Schedule phone calls. Send memes. Send a good morning or goodnight text. Send each other pictures of your outfit for the day. Send each other music. That being said, don't be afraid to branch out a little. Zoe and I have been a unit basically since birth. It's honestly been a little weird having to make friends on my own. It can be a great time to figure out who you are as an individual. Be each other's cheerleader, but don't be each other's crutch. Don't be worried about your twin forgetting about you. You'll always be each other's best friends, no matter what happens. You guys will always have something special that no one else will ever have."

Lisa & Ela

Location: Germany and South Africa
Occupation: Social Workers (and Ela is currently a postgraduate Student for Foundation Phase Teaching)

We are identical twins, but our characters could not be more different! Lisa is more serious and very accurate in everything she does! She is a perfectionist. Ela is more relaxed about things and does not take life too serious especially in situation one can't do anything about anyway.
We trust each other deeply and there are only our significant others who get close to the way how intensely we know each other.

- "[We talk] almost every day! We talk via WhatsApp, we chat via WhatsApp, we video call via WhatsApp! Be ok with missing each other! It doesn't get better! Talk to each other as much as you can and share as much about your life as possible!!! The special twin connection is always there! One feels when something is off even though you live far apart! I make sure that my twin knows that she can call me any time off day or night and so can I call her! Be happy for each other! The most important is that your twin is happy even though if that means you live far apart."

Jenna & Jane

Location: Los Angeles and San Francisco, CA, United States
Occupation: Information Organizer & Talent Researcher and Professional

Home Organizer & Life Coach

Twins are the best. Yes, we also think it's creepy when we say things at the same time. No, we've never switched places. We could never imagine growing up without a twin, and wouldn't trade being twins for anything in the world!

- "No matter how far apart, you never lose your twin connection, and it's been a great opportunity for us to grow as individuals while still having a built-in best friend. Plus, it's fun to look forward to visiting each other, and we *love* being recognized as twins even more because it doesn't happen all the time."

We know that there are plenty of twins who have mentioned that it is too hard to separate and have therefore not done it. But, at least your fellow twins, have shown that it is possible and that the twin bond can survive long-distance. Or as we like to say "Nothing can come betwin us"! Let's move on to our favorite twin moments.

Chapter eight
Favorite twin moments

MOST PEOPLE COME
INTO THIS WORLD ALONE,
I CAME INTO THIS WORLD WITH YOU

TWINNING
store

- **"He's the most golden-hearted person. I think a lot of people spend their life looking for a partner, someone to be a mirror to reflect upon, to remind them that they've lived. You want someone to tell you what he witnessed in your life. My twin brother has always been that for me."**[xiii]

- Scarlett Johansson, actress (Twin brother - Hunter Johansson, actor)

Having known someone your entire life means that you have tons of memories together. Some of our earliest memories we can remember sitting next to each other. There is something special about having someone that knows all the situations you have been in. We like to say "that our twin is more reliable than a diary". Although said jokingly, very few things happen without us being together or at least calling each other first thing after something happened.

Sometimes we find that we can't keep our memories separate from each other. K has definitely told stories that E was the one that experienced and genuinely thinking it was herself. Something that we think is so funny!

Besides the many fun twincations we have had together, our favorite twin moment is probably the day we launched Twinning Store. The nerves and anticipation, and not knowing how people would respond. But luckily, we got positive response right away and we are still pinching ourselves that twins all over the world are connecting with us and that our community is growing on a daily basis.

And the moments keep coming every single time we write a twin meme and post on social media. Us being the only twins in the team (at least for the time being) we never know if what we post is a twin thing or a K&E thing. So, when something we post resonates with the community, we literally get chills (the good kind).

We love that we now get to participate in some amazing twin moments. Through Twinning Store, we have been invited to twin birthday parties, engagement speeches, adoption parties, bachelorette parties, gender reveals, work anniversaries, twincations, Halloween, Thanksgiving and holidays. We also love when photos are shared from the twin moments that happens in day to day life. It makes us so happy to have a sense of community to make those moments even a little more special and celebrated from a twin perspective.

Twinput

What are the favorite twin moments of the #twinfluencer family? Here are some of the answers:

Rachel & Rebekah Aladdin (aka Reine)

Location: Los Angeles, CA, United States

Occupation: Director of Executive Recruiting and Celebrity Make-up Artist

The Aladdin twins, Rebekah and Rachel, are multi-talented twin sisters based out of LA. While Rebekah is a celebrity make-up artist and Rachel, has made a solid career for herself in a completely different industry as a Director of Executive Recruiting. Outside of their everyday careers, they both sing and model.

- "The moments when we're twinning on accident. We have a lot of the same clothes (only a few items), but there have been a few times where we will get dressed separately and arrive to a place wearing the exact same outfit from head to toe!"

Divya & Devyani Biswal

Location: New York City, NY, USA and Ottawa, Canada
Occupation: Dance Majors in College

Divya Biswal is a model and a professional athlete who is training to hopefully make the 2020 Olympics for triple jump representing Canada. Devyani Biswal is doing a Masters in financial math at the University of Ottawa and also training to hopefully represent Canada at the 2020 Olympics in the 100m hurdles.

- "Our favorite twin moment has to be making our first senior international team together. At Nationals, Divya was having a rough time during the triple jump final and Devyani raced the hurdle prelim on the other side of the track. Divya: "I remember looking up on the big screen and seeing that she had qualified for the final and run a personal best. I think I shed a tear of happiness because I've known her struggles with injuries. I then jumped a distance good enough for third place."

Twinning fact - DID YOU KNOW?
The rate of identical twins is universal. It's not impacted by race, nationality or genetics and is about 1 in 285 births.[xiv]

Sam & Kit Wallen Russell

Location: South Bend, IN, United States and Reading, United Kingdom
Occupation: Directors of JooMo Ltd.

Sam is a Nuclear Astrophysicist with a Master's degree from The University of Surrey and Notre Dame University and loves Quantum Mechanics. Kit is a Planetary Geophysicist, with a Master's Degree from UCL and a published Author. We Direct JooMo Ltd. along with our parents, where we talk all over the world about our Research into the Skin Microbiome; our goal is to end the Skin Allergy Epidemic, bringing healthy skin (based on scientific research) and happiness to millions across the world. We are Modern Tennis players where we represented our counties and Universities.

- "We sometimes have muddled memories. So for example, when we were very small, there was an incident where one of us threw a very heavy boules ball at the other's head, but we are both convinced that we are the one that threw it. Consequently, one of us was taken inside by our grandmother, crying our eyes out and with a dent in our head! Very strange though, that neither of us remembers being the victim…"

Isaac & Elijah Bell

Location: Los Angeles, CA, United States
Occupation: Actors

With their fun challenges, comedy skits, and sharing behind the scenes of their modeling and acting careers, the twin brothers have built a loyal following from around the world. Aside from their ever growing YouTube following, the twins are also aspiring actors represented by renowned agencies. In addition, the Bell twins are models who have worked with some of the world's largest brands, such as Nike and Pacsun.

- "Literally every moment together is amazing we have such a strong bond that we can make anything fun together."

From day one twins share moments together. It is so special to have someone to enjoy these moments with. As we get older we may not be there for all the memories in person, but we still share the joy. Some twin moments are more special than others. In the next chapter, we will explore one of the earliest twin moments for twins - birthdays.

Chapter nine
Sharing a birthday

> WHEN YOU ARE USED TO TWO NAMES
> SQUEEZED INTO ONE BIRTHDAY SONG
>
> **TWINNING**
> store

- **"I was born a twin and from the moment I came into this world I had to share it with someone. I shared every birthday, every Christmas, I shared my bedroom, I shared my clothes, I shared everything I had in this world and I didn't know that there was another way because I always had my brother with me."[xv]**

- Ashton Kutcher, actor and investor (Twin brother to Michael Kutcher, advocate and public speaker)

One of the first memories we have is celebrating our birthdays together. In the early years, our mom was diligent in providing two cakes for us. But over the years, we are more accustomed to one. We were curious about this and so we polled 598 twins, 65% percent share a cake and 35% have a cake each. No one reported trouble with the solution of one cake, probably because as twins we are so accustomed to sharing anyways.

There are other unique aspects to sharing a birthday. As twins you become pros at:

- blowing out candles at the same time
- sharing the spotlight
- getting shared birthday greetings
- taking twin sandwich photos (where a non-twin is in the middle and the twins are on each side of the non-twin)
- looking at each other when the song is sung
- and maybe the most unique, looking away from each other when you know you have gotten the same gift. Or opening a shared gift with the same gusto as an individual gift.

Personally, none of this bothers us the slightest. If anything we feel lucky it is that way. E loves celebrating our birthday with big celebrations, whereas K rather have a small dinner. So we usually do both.

We obviously have to touch on the topic of giving gifts to twins. This is a question we often get from non-twins buying gifts for twins and even new twin parents trying to navigate birthdays. Twins are used to getting the same gift, and we are used to sharing gifts. From asking our community, on the whole, it doesn't seem like it is a big deal.

Yes, we will make fun of it, because it is something that we all have experienced time and time again. But, it is the thought that counts and we are just happy that someone cares enough about us to gift us something! P.S. We still even as adults get both shared gifts and same gifts in different colors.

We have yet to come across any twins that resent sharing their birthday, but that is not to say that they don't exist. For us, the reasoning is easy, having the same birthday and celebrating it together is the only thing we remember and we have never questioned it. It wasn't until we started Twinning Store and analyzing twin life that we even thought of it as different!

Twinput

So what are some other perks of sharing a birthday? We asked the #twinfluencer community for their favorite birthday moments:

1. Carly Lewandowski (@Carly_lewandoski), New Jersey, United States:

    - "Being able to sing to someone else during your birthday celebration and not sit there awkwardly during happy birthday songs."

2. Julie Gidney & Nicole Hickson (@gidneyjulie and @hicksonnicole), British Columbia, Canada:

    - "We always have a party partner"

3. Sarah & Lauren Albee (@justplainoldsarah), Whittier, California, United States:

    - "You know you will get something you enjoy since your twin knows you best"

4. Jennifer Brooks, (@Jennifer_brooks_lmt), Fort Worth, Texas, United States:

    - "We have YET another reason to hang out and act silly with each other."

5. Patti Ieraci & Nikkie Munstis (@patti_ieraci and @feedthetraveler5), Connecticut, United States:

    - "Having someone to always celebrate with"

6. Gabriella & Graziella Rossetto (@tipsdagemeas), Brazil:

    - "That even if we don't throw a party, we'll have someone special by our side to celebrate"

7. Hally and Sally (@hallyandsally), Dominican Republic:

    - "That not only one is the center of attention (we are very shy)."

8. Soreeta Glover Hinds & Noreeta Glover Hill (@thebrowncowbakeshopokc and @queenofthepi), Oklahoma City, OK, United States

    - "You'll never have to celebrate alone!"

9. Jolee Oppenheimer (@jaoppenheimer29), FL, United States:

    - "There is always someone as excited about it as I am"

Twinning fact - DID YOU KNOW?:
The scientific study of twins is known as "gemellology".
This kind of study provides valuable information for all sorts of health and psychological research, as twins allows researchers to pull apart genetic and environmental influences.[xvi]

Twins share countless memories together - one that is very unique is sharing our birthday together. Although we never thought of it growing up, we have in the later years understood how special it is. Let's move on twin humor and pranks.

Chapter ten
Twin humor and pranks

TWIN INSIDE JOKES

EVERYBODY ELSE

MY TWIN

TWINNING
store

- **"We played a few pranks on set. But we never swapped characters at work. James and I were always scared to death that if we did, we'd get caught!"**[xvii]

  - Oliver Phelps, actor (and twin brother to James Phelps, actor)

If there is one thing, we have learned from starting Twinning Store, is that twins have a lot of inside jokes. How could you not, when you have shared so much together. When we are around friends and family, we can start laughing with just one stare.

We have also learned that identical or fraternal twins alike know how to do mischievous acts. Some identical twins may trick people with their looks, but fraternal twins definitely do their fair share of pranks too. We don't know where the association between twins and the expression "double trouble" stems from but we definitely think many twins live up to it. Ourselves included!

As mentioned before, when we were born, we never took a test to determine whether we are identical or fraternal, and as an effect we don't know. And although some people can't tell us apart, others may say that we don't even look alike at all. Because of that, we never really dared swapping places. Although we have on occasion stepped in for each other when we know the other person doesn't know us well enough (like at the post office). We do however prank our friends and family from time to time.

One of our favorite things is that we don't have to communicate about doing a prank before we do it. We might start tricking our friend into thinking that we are moving from Los Angeles, and instead of K saying "no, we are not", she will add to the joke making it seem even more believable. Our poor friends!

Twinput

Knowing that there are braver twins than us out there, we asked what pranks the community had been up to and if any of the identical twins have ever used their likeness to their advantage. And their answers make us crack up:

Adriana & Ariana Sanchez

Location: Merced, CA, United States
Instagram handle: @abravenewgirl @airyana_7

- "Switching places in 2nd grade for two weeks.. Until our mom finally caught on!"

Lindsey McVey & Jenna Elkins

Location: Burlington, VT and Nashville, TN, United States
Instagram handle: @lynnsea88 and @jenna.m.elkins

- "Yes! I was a 7th-grade science teacher and was teaching a unit on genetics. I told my students I had successfully cloned myself and then my twin entered the classroom and my students fell out of their chairs! Best prank ever!

Megan & Amanda Morse

Location: New Haven, VT, United States
Instagram handle: (@blazersgirl)

- "Switched classes once in 6th grade. We had sub teachers that day so they didn't know us as well. Unfortunately, it was for reading time. Had no idea what their book was about. It was terrible."

Twinning fact - DID YOU KNOW?
In Germany there was a jewelry thief who managed to steal $6.8 million
worth of jewelry from a luxury department store. He was caught but the police ran into an unexpected problem when they attempted to try him in court. The jewelry thief was an identical twin and the DNA scans weren't able to figure out which of them it was and they were forced to let them both go[xviii]

Gabriella & Graziella Rossetto

Location: Brazil
Instagram: @grazfross

- "I don't know if it's a prank... it's more like an habit: We always pretend to be each other on the phone if one of us is too busy to pick up or text. No one ever noticed, because our voices are very similar!"

Note from K&E: We have totally done this too!!

Tara & Tif Bucknor

Location: Jupiter, FL, United States
Instagram: @taaraanova

- "Sat an exam for my sister - got a D. Needless to say we did not try it again."

The Oscar-winning Rami Malek guested the Jimmy Kimmel show in 2015 and shared a story about him and his twin brother, Sami Malek. Here is what Rami shared:

"So he calls me one day... he goes, 'Hey, do you know a Greek monologue from a Greek tragedy? [I said] 'Yeah, of course, I've just been doing this for four years. He goes, 'Listen, I need you to come down to my university' I need you to do this for my class. It's gonna give me the points I need.' I go, 'Yeah I'm gonna get the points and we're gonna make this happen.' And I deliver this monologue in front of the entire lecture hall and I get applauded, people dig it. And I think the professor starts looking at me kind of accusatory like, 'Where the hell did you come up with that?''

Pranksters or not - twins do have a lot of fun together. We have a life-time of developing our own humor and live up to the expression "double trouble". Some twins are braver in doing pranks than others, and thanks to them we can all laugh a little extra. Next, let us learn more about what it is like to work together as twins.

Chapter eleven
What it is like to work together as twins

MY TWIN WILL TELL ME THE TRUTH,
THE WHOLE TRUTH,
AND NOTHING BUT THE TRUTH...

TWINNING
store

- **"When we started our business way back, we shared a business cell phone. He would have it half the time, then I would take it half the time"[xix]**

   - Jonathan Scott, actor and realtor known for the show Property Brothers (Twin brother to Drew Scott, actor and realtor known for the show Property Brothers)

We have always worked together in some capacity. We got our first job together in our teens and then we founded our first company together in college. Then we went through phases where we worked in different industries, but we have always had a shared project some way or another.

Being two has definitely meant that we have a constant sounding board and each other's encouragement. We have heard from other twins too that having a twin makes a natural co-founder because you are already so in sync.

Starting a business together was a dream of ours since we were kids and that we now have started Twinning Store is definitely a dream come true. Being so close we can read each other's body language and know pretty much what the other person is thinking. This translates into a great work dynamic, which obviously comes in handy in business.

We feel honored by the number of twins that reach out and ask us about advice on how to start a business. And, we know there are many twinpreneurs out there and many others who are considering starting to work together. Therefore, we have put together a list of our top three advice for improving your working relationship:

1. Divide tasks based on interest

The day we accepted that we have slightly different business personalities, we also discovered that our strength lies in fulfilling each other. It is often easier said than done because it takes time to know what work is needed and what work one likes to do. But we did a session where we wrote our interests down and what tasks we were most passionate about.

E loves writing and customer service, K is more into the website development and supply chain. Whereas, one twin likes the initial design phase more than the production side, and so on. From there, we divided up tasks accordingly. We try to revisit this list every so often to see if anything has changed, needs to be added or taken out. With that divide, we have been able to work with more motivation and better results.

2. Force breaks without any business discussion allowed

If you are lucky, you will love what you are doing and will want to work way outside regular business hours. That intensity may sometimes end up in some heated discussions about how things could have been done in different ways. This is normal, you are both working on growing your "baby" and you may look at some things differently.

However, the quicker you learn to give each other the benefit of the doubt and remember that you are working towards the same goal the better (for you and everyone around you). Take some time to cool down and then talk about it. The brain AND your relationship need a break every once in a while. So make sure to spend time together without discussing business. Find it hard to discuss something else than business matters?

Do something completely different: go on a hike, go horseback riding, go swimming, take a cooking class - anything that forces you to focus on the adventure at hand.

3. Trust your twinstinct

The brilliance of being twins in business is that you are not relying on just one gut instinct but two. Use that to your advantage. We don't make decisions if we aren't both on board and it has saved us many headaches. Needless to say, it has started many heated arguments too!

However, we are very skilled at ending the arguments before going in to meetings and not letting our team get stuck in an awkward position on which twin to side with. (There is a more extensive chapter on arguing later in the book)

Twinput

We also asked some other twins who work together what they enjoy about it:

Julie Lancia & Jodie Kammerer

Location: Seattle, WA, and Pleasant Hill, CA, United States
Occupation: Blogger, Photographer, Influencer, Writer, Teacher

We're Jodie & Julie, The Design Twins. We are identical twin sisters who love making friends. We started our journey on Instagram in 2014 and our blog in 2016. We are passionate about decorating, photography, teaching, and connecting with people.

- "We see being twins as a huge asset to our design processes. We have each other to bounce ideas off of. We help each other if we get stuck or have questions. We have HONEST feedback always, someone who we know is never going to hold back, for better or for worse, in order to protect our feelings. People sometimes hear us and think we're somewhat brutal with each other...it's just normal...but it's not how others interact. It's like giving yourself feedback...brutal honesty. We are used to it and it's very helpful."

Armando Soto & Ramón Soto

Location: Phoenix, AZ, United States
Occupation: Owner of Raicesroots and Lead Floral Designer of Flowers by Raicesroots

Armando is the baby of the family as Ramón is three whole minutes older. Armando loves life and is super passionate about family, friends, and owning his own business. Ramón is a dancer and a highly motivated artist who loves his family and friends. His personal goal is to visit all 50 states before he turns 50. They both love being outdoors, sports, and traveling.

- "How would we describe working together? To sum it all up, Armando would simply say, "Passion Worth Sharing." Ramón would say, "Family Oriented Madness!" That's in a positive tone, of course."

Christelle & Daphné Debauve

Location: Brussels, Belgium & New York City, United States
Occupation: Elementary Teacher & Speech therapist/Acupuncturist and both entrepreneurs

Identical twins born in Brussels (Belgium) in 1980, we had a classic twin life from the start, dressed the same up to 11 years old (oh my), looked very much alike and used to fight a lot, A LOT. Always shared the same classroom up to High School graduation but NEVER EVER sat together in class. In 2010, Daphné moved to New York City and still to this day, we live with 6000 Km in between us and with that distance, our lifelong dream to one day work together had to find its way so we started George & Georgette, LLC, a brand of mismatched shoes for kids!

- "We communicate so effortlessly with each other that it's a breeze to work, decide and face problems together. We've been training since birth."

Twinning Fact - DID YOU KNOW?
In a research study conducted by the Institute of General Linguistics, University of Amsterdam, Netherlands, it was found that up to 40% of twins develop their own private language that only they can understand.[xx]

Dawn & Samantha Goldworm

Location: New York City, NY, United States
Occupation: Entrepreneurs

We are identical mirror image twins but our personalities are contrasting yet complementary. Our synethestic abilities are also identical and thus we live in our own perfumed world.

- "Use your twin instinct and connection to lead the way."

Jordan & Loanne Collyer

Location: London, United Kingdom
Occupation: Digital influencers & DJs

We're Jordan and Loanne, identical twin sisters who have grown up by the sea in Portugal with similar interests in travelling, fashion, music and food! We're not only twins but business partners and best friends (worst enemies at times too) but that's only normal!

- "We have capitalized on the fact that we're twins, it's our USP (unique selling proposition) and don't think we would be in the same position today if we weren't working together."

The expression two is better than one applies to a lot of situations with twins, especially when working together. Twins have a head start in life in learning how to communicate, bounce ideas off each other and knowing each other's best qualities. We love learning how other twins solve the challenges that come with it. However, not all twins work together, which is what we will discuss more in the next chapter.

Chapter 12
Taking different directions

THANKFUL FOR MY TWIN

TWINNING
store

- **"Joy and I are very contrasting characters. She never wanted to act, which was quite good because it would have been very competitive between us."[xxi]**

- Eva Green, actress (and twin sister to Joy Green, actress)

Although we work together now, we have also had times that we did completely different things. We also know from a poll we did that around 48% of the twins polled work together and 52% don't work together.

Before we started college, we thought we would go to the exact same things. It wasn't until we started learning about the many career paths that it changed. However, it was a challenge to admit to each other that we weren't in to the same things and that we had to take different directions. It felt scary to have to separate and neither of us wanted to be the first to admit it. But we somehow (neither of us remembers who dared to say it first) ended up going in different directions. Even so much, that we chose to study different topics in different countries. It makes sense, K has always been the more creative and outgoing twin, with E being more analytical and reserved.

After college, we were similarly aiming for careers in different industries. We both started our careers in jobs that suited those aspects of our personalities. Slowly over time, we found more and more ways to work together, and eventually we started Twinning Store and we have roles where we can utilize our characteristics.

We think it is important that twins get the chance to find out what their passions are separate from their twin. Some find out this while together, some needs some distance. But regardless, it can be hard to separate since you have so many shared memories and often shared qualities.

Twinput

We asked two sets of twins on what it is like to go in different directions in terms of careers:

Allie & Lucie Fink

Location: New York, NY, United States
Occupation: Financial Services & Video Producer (respectively)

We are 27-year-old fraternal twins living in New York City! The two of us shared a room for much of our lives growing up, and we also did pretty much everything together (we went to the same summer camp, the same college, and now we live in the same city). We are total best friends and have the most special bond imaginable! Even though we no longer live together (Lucie is married and Allie lives with her boyfriend), we still live relatively close to one another and get together weekly without fail to do yoga, relax together, or cook.

- "We would NOT be able to swap places for a day! Not only do we not look similar enough to 'stand in' for the other, but

Lucie wouldn't know any of the technical aspects of Allie's financial role, and Allie would be a little uncomfortable being on camera all day."

Emma & Kelly Slater

Location: Los Angeles, CA, United States
Occupation: Dancing with the Stars Professional Dancer and Seamstress

The Slater sisters grew up in Tamworth, United Kingdom. They attended school together and though their careers lead them through different forms of education after high school, they now both live happily in Los Angeles.

- "I think people should know that twins can be like a compass. Joined in their center, but have arrows free to look in different directions. Emma and I definitely do with our interests and careers, but as twin sisters I can't deny we both have arrows in the same direction!"

Working together or not doesn't affect the twin bond, but having a twin business partner may be a competitive advantage. We are constantly inspired by other twins and how they live their lives, either doing something together or cheering each other on. But twins don't always agree, which is what the next chapter will discuss.

Chapter 13
Arguing

WHEN YOU ARGUE WITH YOUR TWIN,
BUT THINK OF SOMETHING FUNNY
AND STOP THE FIGHT TO SHARE THE LAUGH

TWINNING
store

- *"Ever since we were little - and this goes from when we were babies through high school - everyone always said, 'The twins are so entertaining. Just sit down with them for five minutes, and you will see so much happen. They will fight, they will laugh, they will love each other, and then they will tell each other off.'"*[xxii]
    - *Brie Bella, retired professional wrestler (Twin sister to Nikki Bella, retired professional wrestler)*

We are infamous for our arguments. The arguments never last long, nor are the topics for our conflicts rarely important, but it happens quite frequent. Our parents and friends close to us know to stay out of it, because by the time they have taken a side, we are either friends again or we will start defending each other.

Not knowing a life without someone makes you close, but not necessarily perfect at communication. In short, we never really learned to filter out some comments that would seem mean or hurtful if said to someone else.

Although we try to keep our arguments hidden from people, our dear friends have witnessed some intense fights. We laugh about it now as many have shared that they thought we would never ever talk to each other again, but then we become friends again within minutes.

Our only rule for fighting is to never let it interfere with business or social events. So more than once, we have sat together in meetings where everyone thinks everything is fine, but we are both thinking of the next thing to say in the argument. Ironically, many times in such meetings people will have asked the standard twin question "Do you ever argue?". Haha - twin problems!

Twinput

We have always wondered if it is the same for other twins, so we interviewed some of our fellow twins and asked about whether they argue:

Joyce & Raissa De Haas

Location: London, United Kingdom
Occupation: Co-founders, Double Dutch Drinks

The identical twin sisters, Joyce and Raissa, behind the UK-based Double Dutch Drinks are revolutionizing the drinks business with their award-winning drinks mixers. Their products are sold in over 22 countries worldwide. The twins have been awarded by Forbes 30 under 30 and won several start-up competitions.

- "Haha, yes we do. But often we have to attend to business or join a meeting mid-fight."

Ezra & Adeev Potash

Location: Los Angeles, CA, United States
Occupation: Musicians and TV Hosts

The twin brothers are the horn players on some of your favorite songs with artists like John Legend, Major Lazer. Diplo and many more. When not on tour you can find them eating and hosting cooking shows on Bravo TV and Travel Channel

- "We literally never argue, sounds crazy but it's true."

Eltoria & Nou

Location: London and Bath, United Kingdom
Occupation: Influencers and YouTubers

Nou and Eltoria are two non-identical twins who live in London, England. Eltoria is known for her addictive unboxing and lifestyle videos on YouTube whilst Nou is a consultant in London (who loves to feature in videos now and again). Eltoria and Nou have recently started up a YouTube channel together called 'Eltoria and Nou' where they vlog about their lives as being twins.

- "We are the kinda twins who would have a full-blown argument over text but then go to the cinema half an hour later as nothing happened!"

Emma & Kelly Slater

Location: Los Angeles, CA, United States
Occupation: Dancing with the Stars Professional Dancer and Seamstress

The Slater sisters grew up in Tamworth, UK. They attended school together and though their careers lead them through different forms of education after high school, they now both live happily in Los Angeles.

- Emma: "We don't argue AT ALL! I mean, I don't even think we used to that much when we were kids, maybe just the normal amount. We just know there's nothing more important than each other, we stand up for each other in every situation. If anyone ever upset her, I would go Liam Neeson crazy on them!

- Kelly: "There are no arguments whatsoever! Not even as kids. We played with different toys so never argued over them. We have different styles and so we never argued about clothes either and we were in the same friendship groups all through school!"

Resolving arguments

Some twins argue, some don't. As we mentioned, our arguments rarely are important and typically an argument is over before people around us have time to take a side. It is also often in the way of us doing something that is more important, like sharing and laughing about something funny.

Twinput

Being curious about how our way of handling arguments differ from other twins, we of course had to ask other twins about how long it takes to make up after an argument:

Alexandra & Andrea

Location: San Diego, CA, United States
Occupation: Founders of We Are Andrex

We are from Miami, FL and living it up in San Diego! We are TWINS! We might look the same, but we are two unique souls. Together we are stronger. And together we are brighter. After expressing how special and lucky we are to be twins, we finally decided it was time to put all our positive energy and passion into jewelry, We Are Andrex *(WAA)* - an accessory in your everyday wardrobe that can remind you that you are loved. WAA shares that special connection and bond you have with someone that will forever be your person.

- "Right away. We may give each other space right after we apologize, but as long as the other twin knows that they are okay then it's all good."

Charlotte & Heather Howard

Location: Bedfordshire, United Kingdom and Perth, Australia

Occupation: International Operations Coordinator and Event Coordinator

We both love to travel and to try new things. We love to have a drink and share the same sense of humor in whatever we do! We are extremely close, argue a lot but always make up within minutes

- Charlotte: "When I meet parents of young twins, the first thing I tell them is that the arguing never gets any better! Heather is living in Australia and I am in the UK but we still speak daily. We also still argue daily and often our video calls end in one of us hanging up on the other. Our friends and family all know never to get involved and within minutes, we have both forgotten all about it. We instinctively defend eachother and have eachother's back if we feel we need to."

Rachel & Rebekah Aladdin (aka Reine)

Location: Los Angeles, CA, United States
Occupation: Director of Executive Recruiting and Celebrity Make-up Artist

The Aladdin twins, Rebekah and Rachel, are multi-talented twin sisters based out of LA. While Rebekah is a celebrity make-up artist and Rachel, has made a solid career for herself in a completely different industry as a Director of Executive Recruiting. Outside of their everyday careers, they both sing and model.

- "It really depends on the argument and how "wronged" one of us feels. Most times we can get over it in just a few minutes. Sometimes it will take a few hours. In our adult years, there have been a few arguments that lasted days - those aren't fun at all!"

Eileen & Gilian Reichert

Location: Playa del Carmen, Mexico
Occupation: Owners of the first Vegan Training studio for women in Playa del Carmen.

We feel very blessed we can experience life together, what everyone is looking for (unconditional real love) we were born with it. We don't know how people go through life without a twin! Oh and we are very passionate about spreading the vegan message in Mexico and helping others get in the best shape of their lives through healthy habits.

- "Oh man, we can be ultra mad at each other and 2 seconds after like nothing happened loving and holding hands... very confusing and weird for some people."

Shanae & Shaniece Cole

Location: Burbank, CA, United States
Occupation: Associate Producer and Casting Producer

Born and raised in Lancaster, Pennsylvania, The Cole Twins have been captivating audiences for years through their creative content, vivacious personalities and bold sense of style. Over the last few years, the twins have partnered and worked with established brands, garnered thousands of views across their social media channels and have a dedicated fan base: just by simply being themselves. In addition to working in front of the camera, Shanae and Shaniece have also worked behind the scenes in various facets of the entertainment industry.

- "We make sure we make up before the day is over. We never hold grudges and at the end of the day we need each other and what we have is so special so nothing should break that bond."

Alyson & Alayna Thibodeaux

Location: LA, United States
Occupation: Account Managers for a non-profit

We are fraternal twins. Alyson is 8 minutes older and she never lets Alayna forget it. We have lived together our entire lives and refer to the day we move apart as our divorce.

- "When it comes to arguing - argue. Let it all out. Then make a joke of it. Makes things 100% better! We have argued our entire lives and within 5 minutes we are looking for each other. We each get on each other's nerves but hey, who doesn't get on their siblings nerves it just comes with it. I annoy her. She annoys me. We just work it out. It's a really loving relationship "

Emily & Lyla Allen

Location: Buffalo, NY, United States
Occupation: Students, but we manage our blog and cookbook endeavors

We are high school twins who not only love to cook, but love that we get to do it with each other. Having a twin makes it easy to balance our school work and spread our love of healthy, whole eating.

> - "I would say let arguments go because not having a twin would be awful. Be nice to each other and make sure to make up your own code - Lyla and I have and it is a lot of fun!"

Communicating as much as twins do, we think it must be inevitable that friction must occur from time to time. That doesn't mean, however, that we don't strive to be more mature and argue less. We are personally taking all our fellow twins' advice to heart. Now let's move on to some things that twin parents thinks you should know about twins.

Chapter fourteen
What you should know about twins

TWINMAGGEDON
= WHEN TWO TWINS FIGHT
AND MAKE UP AFTER 10 MINUTES

TWINNING
store

- **"Of course, I can tell them apart"**[xxiii]
  - *Roger Federer, tennis player and father of two sets of twins*

We of course had to ask some friends and family of twins about what they think people should know about twins. As much as we are used to the endless twin questions, we know they are too.

Who better to ask than our own parents? Here is what they said when they were asked in an interview we did with a magazine:
- "The twin bond is just something else and so special. One of the things we always say is that in heated discussions, don't take a stand, because 5 minutes later they will agree."

Twin parent input

We of course had to ask other twin parents too about what they think people should know about twins, especially their own twins:

Twin parents of Chloe & Lily

Location: Burleson, TX, United States
Occupation: Pre-K Students

Chloe and Lily are our twin girls who are so rambunctious and loving. Chloe loves Unicorns and animals with all her heart. Lily loves all things superheroes and wants to be Captain America one day.

- "I think the thing that fascinates me the most is just how alike and different they are at the same time. We have fraternal twin girls. They both have personalities on the opposite ends of the spectrum from each other but at the same time they enjoy doing the same things together and play together."

Cheryl Lage

Location: Richmond, VA, United States
Occupation: Author of Twinspiration: Real-Life Advice from Pregnancy Through the First-Year and Beyond (c. 2016, Taylor Trade)

Twin mom of Darren and Sarah. Cheryl Lage is a true pioneer when it comes to sharing twin life insights online. She was among the first to create a twin support forum back in 2004. The forum later morphed into her current blog Twinfatuation.com. Cheryl has also written not just one, but two (!) books on twins - with all these great accomplishments, her work has become the go-to source for twin parents all over the world.

- "I do think there is WAY too much assumption all twins speak their own language and/or display a mythic bond from birth. So many new twin moms have emailed/contacted me concerned their babies are somehow "defective" twins---or that as stretched-thinly moms, they've not mothered their two "correctly" when their twins don't show signs of supernatural connection from the get-go. From an infant development point-of-view, babies are entirely self-revolving for quite some time. My fondest hope is that new twin mamas would be more merciful with themselves. A close-second myth I'd love to see dispelled is the belief that in every twin pair one is the "smart one" (implying the other isn't), "good one" (meaning the other isn't), or "your favorite" (as if you couldn't have two)!"

Travis & Lynn Durham

Location: Greenville, SC, United States
Occupation: Accountant

They live and work in the Greenville area. They're into lots of things - sports, science fiction, comic books. Lynne loves interior decorating and hanging out with friends. The boys love playing outside, and school (hopefully that stays that way). They just moved into their forever home about a year ago and so far, so good.

- "As their parents, we can tell them apart pretty easy, even if no one else can. We were so worried at birth that we left ribbons on their ankles. But we realized we could see the small differences."
-

Twinning fact - DID YOU KNOW?
While obviously not everyone has an identical twin, according to experts, it could be true that everyone has a doppelganger. Experts credit this to the limited number of genes that influence facial features.[xxiv]

Darlene Brisse

Location: Fort Lauderdale, FL, United States
Occupation: Stay at home mom

Darlene is a stay at home mom to Alessandra & Richard. Their days are full of adventure they love exploring together. Although at times she feels like the third wheel (twin moms know the feeling) and they definitely don't mind the alone time. She loves carpool karaoke with her twins. They always let her be the lead singer, they play their air guitar and pretend drums.

- "Not all twins are identical! "No my boy and girl twins are not identical". It's hard for people to understand that although they were born the same day they are two very different little humans.

Coco Goytizolo

Location: Fort Lauderdale, FL, United States
Occupation: Insurance Adjuster

Twin dad to daughter Ella Starr and son Santiago Philip. We are a unique family who faced a lot of adversity early on. We believe in the power of love. We are in this world for a purpose and to make our lives memorable by giving the best of us.

- "They always have each other's backs; they are very protective of each other. Their connection even when they are mad with each other or when they are apart. It fascinates me their connection, without talking to each other, I can see that they are connected spiritually and that makes my heart smile."

Now we have heard from some of the ones that typically know twins from the youngest age. But what is it like to enter the twin bond later in the life of a twin? In the next chapter, we will explore what it is like to date a twin.

Chapter fifteen
Dating a twin

ALL I WANT IS SOMEONE
WHO CAN HANDLE ALL THE TIME
MY TWIN OCCUPIES

TWINNING
store

- **"I feel we will always have a deeper connection and we can read each other without saying anything. I don't know if that is because we have spent so much time together our entire lives or because we are twins."[xxv]**
    - *Peyton List, actress (and twin sister to Spencer List, actor)*

Among the most frequently asked questions we get from twins and non-twins alike is "what is like to date a twin?". What it is like to be a newcomer to the twin relationship? It is not a secret that the twin bond is strong and so how does it feel to be added to that dynamic?

Personally, we admire significant others of twins. Having grown up with twin questions, the arguing, the excessive communication and so on, we know it can be overwhelming for anyone to enter the twin world. And we know that one's twin can be a *tough* crowd to win over. It is after all our best friend and twin time we are protecting. We are always in awe of how our significant others handle our arguments and know not to take side even if we are practically begging them to.

Our personal advice to anyone dating a twin would be:

- **In an argument, don't take sides**
    - We may ask you to do it, but don't fall for it. The argument will eventually blow over and if you do take sides, we will most likely side with each other. It is weird and illogical, but we are very defensive of each other, even when arguing.
- **Accept that we will be in constant contact**
    - As you may have learned in the chapter about communicating, we talk to each other in some shape or form 24/7. It is just the way it is. You can try to stop it, but we wouldn't recommend it.
- **Learn to appreciate us spending a lot of time together**
    - That means you have more time to spend doing what you want to do. And if you have to cancel on plans, we don't care as we always have each other. It is actually kind of a win-win!
- **Don't say something bad about the twin**
    - This may seem like the most obvious advice. But don't forget this one. It is by far the easiest and quickest way to start a fight EVER!

Twinput

We asked a set of fellow twins about their experience with dating and this is what they had to say:

Lulu & Lala

Location: New York City, NY, United States
Occupation TV & radio personalities for iHearRadio in NYC, Miami and Fort Myers

We are super energetic Latinas who love life and love to entertain and make people smile. Our twin bond is close and we absolutely love to embrace it.

- "There have been times where a boyfriend tries to come between us and that's never going to happen. It takes a great person to understand the bond that twins have with each other."

Us twins are only half the equation about knowing what is it like to date twins. The true experts are the brave souls that decide to enter the twin universe. We say that with a humorous tone, but we do know it can be challenging to date a twin and learn to navigate all the unique aspects of our close-knit relationship with each other.

Input from significant others of twins

We decided that we needed to ask some people that have dated or are married to twins on what their advice is. These four generously offered their input:

Chad Hatcher

Location: McKinney, TX, United States
Occupation: Owner of Xtreme Heights

My wife's name is Terra Hatcher and her sister's name is Donna Houchen. When I first met my wife, I actually didn't know that she and her sister were twins. I thought her sister was way younger. After I found out I never thought it was weird because they both had different personalities but just looked the same.

- "It's always fun hanging out with both of them at the same time. They have a great relationship and we all get along so whenever we hang out, we always have fun. Just go along for the ride. They will talk 24 hours a day, 7 days a week and they might always be together but it's an amazing bond they share and if you are lucky enough you can be a part of it as well."

Nazar

Location: Sacramento, CA, United States
Occupation: Nursing Student

I am married to Irina, who's twin sister's name is Alina. I had known my wife and her twin sister for many years before I started dating her, so the fact that she was a twin was already familiar to me. It was clear to me by the time I considered dating her that she was unique, even compared to her twin. In my mind, I was dating an exceptional woman who happened to be a twin rather than the other way around.

- "My best advice to other significant others of twins is to appreciate your partner for who she is. Be intentional about not developing a habit of comparing her to her own twin - it can be detrimental to you, to her, and to your relationship. She is an individual. Additionally, twins will often have such a close relationship that their significant others might feel threatened by that level of intimacy. I would suggest not to discourage that closeness but instead celebrate it. DO NOT make her choose between her twin or you - 9 times out of 10, you'll fall short and be left in the dust."

Stuart Chapman

Location: Berkshire, United Kingdom
Occupation: Insight Manager

Stuart is married to Amy Chapman, and her twin sister is Emma Walker. My wife is my bestest and most brilliant friend, but dating a twin means spending probably more time than normal with my sister in law and I think that means you end up a lot closer. I think I probably care about my sister in law more than most would, and that's not because she is the same as my wife, in fact very different, but because she is genuinely one of my best friends who I absolutely love spending time with and who I value a lot.

- "Worst [about dating a twin] sounds bad, I would say one of the drawbacks is that my wife and her twin are so close that they often share more than other siblings and maybe that means I get less shared with me. Eg they will discuss things in length and then I just get the highlights. Also, they have to share everything, which means talking at least one hundred gazillion times a day. Just go with it and enjoy the ride. There are obviously some quirks, like needing to be in constant contact and talk about EVERYTHING, but in general it's pretty good. Just always approach from behind with caution, unless one has a different haircut or is massively fatter. Don't let them share clothes either, that's asking for trouble."

Stephen Schlumpf

Location: Lexington, KY, United States
Occupation: Merchandise Service Team (Lowe's)

Stephen is married to wife is Leslie Schlumpf, and her twin sister is Jessica Mueller. We have been married for a little over 2 years. Before getting married Leslie's parents tried explaining what life would be like marrying a twin. They said when you marry one, you marry the other. It's like when people tell you when you marry someone, you marry their family. That statement could not be more true. Jessica and her family hold a special place in our hearts because of their twin bond.

- "I was a little nervous when I found out she is a twin because I didn't want to be tested to see if I knew who was who, but since they aren't identical, it wasn't too difficult. The best part about my wife being a twin is being a part of her family. I get to know more about her brothers and their families but I am closer to my wife's husband. That way when they want to hang out just the two of them, he and I can hang out and get to know one another. Accept that the two of them have inside secrets and jokes that you just won't get haha."

Dating anyone comes with a set of challenges, so dating a twin is no different. We admire and are so grateful to our significant others who are willing to enter our twin relationship as we know we are a lot to handle. Hopefully with the above advice from both sides, we can all learn to be more accepting of each other's starting point. Now on to what it is like to be expecting twins and how twin parents view the twin bond.

Chapter sixteen
Twin parent perspectives

I DIDN'T CHOOSE THE TWIN LIFE,
THE TWIN LIFE CHOSE ME

TWINNING
store

- **"The doctor says, you see that right there, that little grain of rice? That's the baby. You see this other little grain of rice over here? That's the other baby, I was like 'What.' I started laughing hysterically. I just laughed out loud, I couldn't believe it. And that's how I found out I was having twins."**[xxvi]

- Jennifer Lopez, actress and singer about her twins, Emme & Max

When our parents were expecting, social media was not around. So no documentation exists of the time they found out that they weren't expecting one but two babies. We can't imagine the shock when the doctor told them that they were going to be twin parents. From their recollection, it was quite the surprise when the doctor saw two of us on the ultrasound.

Our parents had time to prepare, but we know plenty of twin parents that got the news at the birth. Regardless, twin parenting fascinate us. How do you tackle two and all the nuances that come with twin life? Having gotten to know so many twin parents around the world through Twinning Store, our admiration and respect for raising twins has just grown. And it feels appropriate to dedicate a chapter to them and their insights.

Input from twin parents

We asked two twin parents how they reacted when they found out about expecting twins, here is what they had to say:

Erica Elizarraraz

Location: Los Angeles, CA, United States
Occupation: Merchandise Director

Twin mama to Penelope and Emma Elizarraraz. Born and raised in So-Cal and now living just outside LA. I had my fraternal twin girls in 2015 after trying many years to conceive. It was a long journey, but worth every minute and I wouldn't change a thing. I work as the Merchandise Director for an apparel company. In addition, I blog in my spare time, which is my escape - I truly enjoy engaging with other mamas.

- "The fact that there was not only one of them but TWO. I kept thinking to myself when I was pregnant "how am I going to manage two tiny humans at the.same.time? " Up until I was around 5 months pregnant I was scared so scared."

Mike Davis

Location: New York City, NY, United States
Occupation: Real Estate Agent

I am a real estate broker in NY City on the 'Mike & Marta' Team at Compass. I'm also a proud husband and father of twins: Jack & Amelie.

- "Fear got the worst of me. I feared the worst for some reason believing maybe they'd be born with some health complications. I also had no idea how to make it work. So money and fear of financial security is also up there. But then friends reminded me that our parents and their parents figured it out. People from all around the world figure it out -- no matter what their economic situation."

Twin personalities

- *"They're just completely different personalities. My daughter will be like 'sit down' and he will sit."*
  - George Clooney, actor about his twins Ella & Alexander

People always say that our personalities seem so similar yet so different. Therefore, we had to ask our community if they feel that their personalities differ or not. We did a poll where we asked "Is your personality different to your twin's?" and 67% said yes.

Insight from twin parents

Who could know the difference or similarities better than parents? We asked some twin parents from the #twinfluencer community about their twins' personalities and here is what they had to say:

Twin parents of Chloe & Lily

Location: Burleson, TX, United States
Occupation: Pre-K Students :)

Chloe and Lily are our twin girls who are so rambunctious and loving. Chloe loves Unicorns and animals with all her heart. Lily loves all things superheroes and wants to be Captain America one day.

- "I think the thing that fascinates me the most is just how alike and different they are at the same time. We have fraternal twin girls that are almost 3 years old. They both have personalities on the opposite ends of the spectrum from each other but at the same time they enjoy doing the same things together and play together."

Twinning fact - DID YOU KNOW?
The average time between delivering the first and second twin is 17 minutes[xxvii]

Leah McQueen

Location: Bondi Beach, Sydney, Australia
Occupation: Photographer

Twin mom to Alexander & Zachary McQueen. We have recently moved back to Australia after living in London for 10 years so the boys could experience an Australian lifestyle; beaches, summer and a relaxed environment. We spend our free time doing lots of outdoor activities at the beaches and playgrounds and parks. Alexander and Zachary started full time Daycare last year and are both enjoying learning new things in preparation for starting school in 2021.

- "The way they communicate with each other, through noises and words (twin language) and how my boys sleep with their heads tilted at exactly the same angle when they are napping in their stroller everyday! Everyone comments on this whenever they see them asleep. They are very different, even though they look similar (they are not identical) and have very similar interests. One of my boys enjoys being alone (at times) and is quite grumpy/moody when he wakes up, whereas the other one is totally the opposite!"

Greg and Rachel Pinn

Location: Dallas, TX, United States
Occupation: Product Development and Freelance Copywriter

Greg and Rachel Pinn make a great parenting team because they're a balanced combination of right brain and left brain intelligence, respectively. Greg is a computer engineer and problem solver while Rachel is a creative and therefore a problem creator, so to speak. Together they enjoy the challenge of raising their identical twin girls now that said twins are a bit less high maintenance (read: out of diapers and into kindergarten). Recommendations for other twin parents include signing up for Amazon Subscribe & Save, and making sure you've got a solid sense of humor.

- "Watching them develop their own skills, likes, dislikes, and personalities has been fascinating. They are growing into two unique individuals with a very close bond that we'll never fully understand."

Thomas Jezequel

Location: Malta
Occupation: EU Civil Servants

I'm a 38-year-old French guy from Brittany, married to a Hungarian woman, Judith, and I'm the father of two 5 years old fraternal twin boys, raised bilingually (FR/HU). They were born in Brussels, but we moved to the Mediterranean island of Malta, so they will be schooled in English.
I work for an EU institution.

- "How they can be born at the same time, educated similarly by the same parents, exposed to the same stimulus at the same time.... and be so freakily different. From the moment they were in neo-natal care, we could see differences in characters. This has not changed since. It's not one size fit all, we have to adapt our behaviour to each child, they're not one package. It's easy to forget sometimes. It also fascinates me how they respond to each other behavioural change, especially in the early years. If one starts to crawl, or walk, the other follows. If one starts to talk, the other gets to it. It's not always the same "leader" / "follower", but they progress at the same rhythm because of constant exposure to another kid going through the same phases."

The twin bond

> THE TWIN BOND IS STRONGER THAN JAMES BOND
>
> **TWINNING** store

- "My son said to his brother 'Tristan hold my hand so you don't get eaten by a crocodile'"
  - Chris Hemsworth, actor about twin sons Tristan & Sasha

    The twin bond is something our parents say always has been a part of our existence. We don't know if there is a stronger bond with twins than other siblings, but whatever it is, it is special. A lot of people, living the twin life or not, share this fascination, so we always try to ask twin parents about how they see the twin bond playing out with their twins.

Insight from twin parents

We asked some twin parents in the #twinfluencer community about the twin bond, here is what they had to say:

Courtney El-Ghoul

Location: Northern VA, United States
Occupation: Stay at home mom and Montessori Pre-K teacher for Nahla and Ava

Before becoming a mother of twins, I was an Executive Sales Manager for a Fortune 500 Company. I was truly a workaholic. Selling houses was my number one focus. After having the girls everything changed so rapidly. I decided that staying at home with them was my new number one and I feel really fortunate that this was an option for our family.

- "Hands down, it is special the twin bond they have. It is so crazy! A great example: when they first started preschool... we put them in separate classrooms. But, their teachers would tell me that one of them would ask to go to the bathroom, the other would like... "realize" it and then ask to go as well. Same if one of them was crying, the other would sense it and ask to check on them. It's a connection even if they aren't physically in the same room. I'll never understand it, and I'll never stop being fascinated with it."

Katelyn Halko

Location: Madison, WI, United States
Occupation: Author/Teacher/Mother

Katelyn Halko is a former elementary teacher and current mom to three boys - her oldest Grant, and twins Alex & Ben. As author of "Two Boring Twin Brothers", she was inspired to begin writing by the true life shenanigans of her three boys. She hopes to bring humor to everyday experiences that come with raising children.

- "My twins' bond has been a really special thing to watch. From the moment they were born, they've been a comfort to each other. We'd sleep them next to each other and they'd snuggle and hold hands. They've been best buddies their whole lives and, at only two years old, they know the little ways to make the other one laugh. They also know how to push each other's buttons and have started fighting a bit more. But even on their worst days of toddler fights, you can still see their bond for each other. The minute one of them is sad or gets hurt, the other stops what he's doing to retrieve a cold pack for an injury, or the other's favorite stuffed animal that goes everywhere with him."

We are in awe of twin parents every single day. We know we were more than a handful and we know some of our fellow twins are as well. It is amazing to hear twin parents share their parenting insights and how they see their twins and the twin bond growing and developing. As with everything twin related, all journeys are different, but we love learning about when certain things, such as the twin bond and it show ups. Thank you, twin parents for what you do! The twin world needs you!

In the next and final chapter, twins will share advice with fellow twins.

Chapter seventeen
Advice from twins to other twins

> BEING A TWIN IS LIKE BEING
> A VIP MEMBER IN A CLUB WITH
> ONLY TWO MEMBERS
>
> **TWINNING**
> store

- **"Society tends to always make multiples - whether it's twins or triplets or whatever - one person. And it's not always fair. I encourage multiples to embrace their individual uniqueness because, just as you are an amazing unit together, that can only happen when you are strong individually."** [xxviii]

- Tia Mowry-Hardrict, Actress (and twin sister to Tamera Mowry-Housley, Actress)

One of the most incredible things with building and being a part of a community is realizing how much we can learn from each other. Almost every day, someone shares an advice that we take to heart. We didn't think we could get closer or even more proud of being twins, but we have.

One of the main reasons for us writing this book, is that we wish we had one like this growing up. We didn't have any other twins to consult, nor did we necessarily have the knowledge and experience to know if something was a twin problem or normal problem. We wish we had the expertise of the #twinfluencer community.

Our own relationship gets stronger every single day because the ways twins all over the world share their knowledge. It is so awesome to see that some twins might be embarrassed by being twins, but then others encourage them to be proud and flaunt it. We hope that all twins can be grateful for being born twins and learn to appreciate both the ups and downs that come with it.

There are many things one can do to strengthen the twin relationship. This is our personal advice:

1. Don't assume that because you are twins that you share the same personality

This advice might seem obvious, but it is not necessarily always easy to remember. When you rarely get "breaks" from someone, it is natural to think that you observe and experience things the same. For example, every time we go on twincation, K will be frustrated with E and her lack of organizing her luggage. K prefers a lot of structure, while E prefers (or at least is better at) an organized mess. After hours of battles, we decided to let go of our frustrations, put pen to paper and write down processes that we both can follow.

2. Don't take twin life for granted

You lucked out with a twin, which is unique and special. We get it, your twin can be annoying at times, and sometimes we also have had times we have been distant and going in different directions. But at the end of the day, twin life is truly special and shouldn't be taken for granted. Find ways to celebrate your twin and do it often!

3. Make a twin bucket list

We have so many mutual dreams and goals and a life-time to make them happen. It is so fun to check off the things once it has been done (like flying a small plane or go horseback riding in Montana). It is also a great way to plan out things and make sure you get quality twin time in. We would love to see your twin bucket list. (Please share with us by emailing book@twinningstore.com).

Twinput

We have benefited so much from fellow twins giving us advice. And we are lucky as we pretty much learn something new from twins every single day. Here is some of our favorite advice:

Jennifer & Ashley Rubin

Location: San Francisco, CA, United States
Occupation: Owners of Native Twins Coffee & Native Twins Granola

Jen and Ash are identical mirror image twins from Mill Valley, CA. Best friends and business partners. Jen was born 7 minutes first, she's a lefty and a tomboy at heart, leader of the pack, she's always got her game face on. Ashley is right handed and a girly girl at heart, she's the bubbly one, always smiling and laughing. They balance each other out and make a great team as the dynamic duo!

- "You will be compared in every way almost every day, don't take it too personally"

Lucy Knott & Kelly Sharpe

Location: Stockport, United Kingdom
Occupation: Teaching Assistants, Bloggers and Authors

We are former professional Wrestlers who love all things Italy, Food & Books. When not working with children we adore writing; Lucy writes romance novels, Kelly writes children's books. We love spending time with family & each other & being twins is one of our favorite things! :)

- "It's ok to be your own person. When people tend to think you are the same it can be hard to break free from that idea and feel comfortable being you when you're always being compared to your twin. We love each other more than anything, love being together and are proud to be 'the twins', but it's nice having your own identity too. That can take a little time to figure out, but don't be afraid of it."

Jonta' & Jamison Harris

Location: Los Angeles, CA, United States
Occupation: Digital Marketing and Fashion Experts

With their amazing style and fashion sense, Jonta and Jamison Harris, aka the Harris twins, have built up a worldwide following of people carefully paying attention to the twin brothers' moves. In addition, the twin brothers are digital media experts and have a website filled with great advice and tips.

- "If there was any advice we wish we would have received from other twins growing up it would have been that it's so important to gain our sense of individually. Now that we are older we see how important it is to have our own identity as twins. We would have loved hearing from other twins that it's okay to have differences within our "Twindom."

Jonathan & Joshua Baker

Location: Los Angeles, CA, United States
Occupation: Commercial and movie directors

Originally from Australia, the twin brothers are known as TWIN in the commercial world and as The Baker Brothers in the movie world. The Australian born pair moved to the US in 2007, and have made a name for themselves making commercials for companies such as Nike and Beats by Dre, and movies with actors such Zoë Kravitz, Dennis Quaid, and Michael B. Jordan.

- "The 'twinsult' is something we've come across since primary school. Essentially it's people who are lazy and who don't take the time to learn how to tell us apart. They used to call us 'the twinnies", which drove us insane. We've had people in our lives that we've known for years who say "you're identical, it's impossible to tell you apart!", but it's really on them that they haven't taken the time to get to know us as individuals. It's really not that hard."

Allie & Lucie Fink

Location: New York, NY, United States
Occupation: Financial Services and Video Producer

We are 27-year-old fraternal twins living in New York City! The two of us shared a room for much of our lives growing up, and we also did pretty much everything together (we went to the same summer camp, the same college, and now we live in the same city). We are total best friends and have the most special bond imaginable! Even though we no longer live together (Lucie is married and Allie lives with her boyfriend), we still live relatively close to one another and get together weekly without fail to do yoga, relax together, or cook.

- "We think the biggest misconception about twins is that all twins feel competitive and hate being grouped together constantly. We shared every single birthday party for our whole lives, we went to the same high school, camp and college, and we even borrowed clothes...yet we never felt that sense of competition or that need to be separated. We actually found that the closer we were to one another physically, the more we were emotionally able to branch out, find our own 'thing' and build our own spaces. It's like the dependency paradox; we always knew the other was right there, so we felt more comfortable branching out. If we hadn't gone to college together, we probably would have been constantly texting and calling the other and wouldn't have explored as much on campus."

Heidi & Kristen

Location: Minneapolis, MN, United States
Occupation: RN Care Coordinator and Lease Closing Specialist

We grew up in Wisconsin, went to college in different states and then both ended up in Minneapolis, MN. We've always taken our own paths, but have found a way to be involved in each other's lives.

Heidi has a Wheaten Terrier and works as an RN Care Coordinator and Kristen has a Beagle mix, works as a Lease Closing Specialist and lives with her husband and new baby girl.

- "We wish we had been told to always appreciate being a twin, even when you are tired of having them around."

Carmen & Camille Thomas

Location: Los Angeles, CA, United States
Occupation: Musicians

We are Canadian twins living in LA who write and play music together. Camille plays guitar, Carmen plays flute and we love harmonizing. We believe in spreading love and kindness through who we are as people and through our music.

- "We didn't really know a lot of twins growing up but the advice that would have been cool to know and that maybe someone can hear from us now is to embrace your similarities and your differences. You will be compared to each other but that is okay. You each bring something to the table!"

Alyson & Alayna Thibodeaux

Location: LA, United States
Occupation: Account Managers for a non-profit

We are fraternal twins. Alyson is 8 minutes older and she never lets Alayna forget it. We have lived together our entire lives and refer to the day we move apart as our divorce.

- "Being a twin is just a club that only a select few get to be a part of. Embrace it. Never be ashamed of it. People are fascinated with twins. Let them be fascinated."

All twins are unique in their own way, but we often share many of the same experiences. Just knowing that someone else has gone through a similar situation can often be comforting. By sharing ups and downs with each other through our platform, we know personally, as well as for many others, that we have learned more about twin relationship. We love that younger generations of twins can learn from older generations, and that vice versa can happen too.

Chapter eighteen

Epilogue

This book has been the grandest project that we ever have undertaken and we are thrilled that it is in your hands. We feel so fortunate to be a part of a growing community of twins all over the world. This book wouldn't be possible without the amazing the twinsights shared with us so generously on a daily basis.

Our goal is always to share what advice and education we get with you, and with this book we have finally found a more extensive way to do so.

There is so much more that we could cover, but we will save that for upcoming books. If you feel something needs to be expanded on, please feel free to reach out to us at book@twinningstore.com. We hope that this is only one of several books to come.

Our hope is that you similarly to us have found this book useful, educational and inspiring. Learning about other twins and how they handle twin life has made us more appreciative and accepting of each other.

If you have enjoyed *The Life of Twins*, we hope you consider reviewing it on Amazon and/or Goodreads. This way we hope as many twins as possible around the world will have the opportunity to join in on the fun.

Acknowledgements

There are so many people who have helped us make this book a reality and we are beyond thankful and grateful.

To the over 120 twins, friends and family who have contributed with insights - thank you for generously sharing your time and perspective. Without your point of view *The Life of Twins* would not be as extensive and diverse. This book would not be possible without you and we love that it is a collective effort of twins, friends and family of all ages and from all corners of the world.

Thank you to each and every #twinfluencer. If you had told us back in 2017, that we would have this amazing community as our part of our family, we would have been able to grasp it. Thank you for being our source of inspiration and for pushing us to grow every single day. It is also beyond moving to us to think twins worldwide have given us the chance to serve the twin community in the way we do.

To our professor who made writing fun and who's twin granddaughters keep inspiring us - thank you for everything.

To our amazing editor - thank you for your patience and countless hours making sense of our many changes and script versions.

Lastly, thank you to our friends and family who have supported us from the day we clicked launch on twinningstore.com. Many people would have shaken their heads, but you have kept encouraging us and reminding us that twins need a platform to be celebrated and to connect with each other.

Twin love from us to you.
Xoxo,

INDEX

[i] Madrigal, A. (2014). *There Really Are So Many More Twins Now*. [online] The Atlantic. Available at: https://www.theatlantic.com/health/archive/2014/04/1-million-extra-twins-have-been-born-in-the-last-31-years/360849/

[ii] Bundchen, G. (2018). *Lessons*. Penguin Publishing Group.

[iii] Dios, J. (2012). *Mirror Mirror: Examining Nature's Copy and Paste*. [online] Scientific American Blog Network. Available at: https://blogs.scientificamerican.com/guest-blog/mirror-mirror-examining-natures-copy-and-paste/

[iv] En.m.wiktionary.org. (2019). *twin - Wiktionary*. [online] Available at: https://en.m.wiktionary.org/wiki/twin

[v] Binkley, C. (2018). *Mary-Kate and Ashley Olsen's The Row Launches Menswear*. [online] WSJ. https://www.wsj.com/articles/mary-kate-and-ashley-olsens-the-row-launches-menswear-1535371228

[vi] Oceana Canada. (n.d.). *Ten Fascinating Facts about Polar Bears*. [online] Available at: https://www.oceana.ca/en/blog/ten-fascinating-facts-about-polar-bears

[vii] Seventeen. (2016). *The Heartbreaking Reason Tamera Mowry Thought She Was the "Ugly Twin" on "Sister, Sister"*. [online] Available at: https://www.seventeen.com/celebrity/news/a39611/the-heartbreaking-reason-tamera-mowry-thought-she-was-the-ugly-twin-on-sister-sister/

[viii] Cragg, M. (2015). *The Veronicas: 'People ask where we met ... we say "the womb"'*. [online] the Guardian. Available at: https://www.theguardian.com/culture/2015/mar/11/the-veronicas-interview-jessica-lisa-origliasso-billy-corgan

[ix] Contributor, C. (2018). *Countries With Most Twins Identified*. [online] livescience.com. Available at: https://www.livescience.com/16469-twins-countries-twinning-rates.html [Accessed 10 Dec. 2019].

[x] Harper's BAZAAR. (n.d.). *Grace Kelly's Daughter-in-Law Says Raising Twins Is "Exhausting"*. [online] https://www.harpersbazaar.com/celebrity/latest/a29990914/princess-charlene-monaco-raising-twins-interview/

[xi] Wired To Be Social: the Ontogeny Of Human Interaction
Umberto Castiello-Cristina Becchio-Stefania Zoia-Cristian Nelini-Luisa Sartori-Laura Blason-Giuseppina D'Ottavio-Maria Bulgheroni-Vittorio Gallese - https://www.ncbi.nlm.nih.gov/pubmed/20949058

[xii] Fetal Doppler (twins) - R. Griffin - https://www.webmd.com/baby/doppler-twins

[xiii] Scarlett Johansson in Black and White
Dotson Rader - https://parade.com/392244/dotsonrader/scarlett-in-black-and-white/

[xiv] Twinsuk.co.uk. (n.d.). *10 Amazing Facts About Twins | Multiple Birth Statistics, Facts & Trivia | Twin Tips | Resources Centre | Twins UK*. [online] https://www.twinsuk.co.uk/twinstips/18/9934235/multiple-birth-statistics,-facts

&-trivia/10-amazing-facts-about-twins/

[xv] Ashton Kutcher Becomes Emotional Talking About His Twin Brother Emmy Griffiths - https://www.hellomagazine.com/celebrities/2017041038029/ashton-kutcher-becomes-emotional-talking-about-his-twin-brother/

[xvi] Why Twin Studies?" *Michigan State University Twin Research*, msutwinstudies.com/why-twin-studies.

[xvii] Cosmopolitan. (2017). Did Fred and George Weasley ever swap roles on Harry Potter? An investigation. [online] Available at: https://www.cosmopolitan.com/uk/entertainment/a13936616/fred-george-weasley-swap-roles/ [Accessed 12 Dec. 2019].

[xviii] Berlin, Claudia Himmelreich /. "Despite DNA Evidence, Twins Charged in Heist Go Free." *Time*, Time Inc., 23 Mar. 2009, content.time.com/time/world/article/0,8599,1887111,00.html.

[xix] Hohman, Maura. "Property Brothers Reveal They Will Star in New Sitcom on FOX Based Off Their Book." *PEOPLE.com*, 30 Nov. 2018, people.com/home/property-brothers-to-star-in-new-sitcom-fox-based-off-book/

[xx] Bakker, P. "Autonomous Languages of Twins." *Acta Geneticae Medicae Et Gemellologiae*, U.S. National Library of Medicine, 1987, www.ncbi.nlm.nih.gov/pubmed/3434134.

[xxi] Ruffini, Karen. "Stars You Had No Idea Were Twins." *TheList.com*, The List, 26 Sept. 2019, www.thelist.com/91317/stars-idea-twins/.

[xxii] Lengel, Kerry. "Bella Twins in WWE Live in Phoenix." *Azcentral*, 18 Mar. 2015, www.azcentral.com/story/entertainment/events/2015/03/18/diva-brie-bella-wwe-live-phoenix/24914519/.

[xxiii] Nast, C. (2019). *73 Questions With Roger Federer*. [online] Vogue. Available at: https://www.vogue.com/article/73-questions-with-roger-federer [Accessed 9 Nov. 2019].

[xxiv] "Does Everyone Have a Look-Alike?" LiveScience, Purch, www.livescience.com/52103-does-everyone-have-a-look-alike.html.

[xxv] "Peyton List Tells Sweety High How She and Twin Brother Spencer Are Basically Telepathic." *Sweety High*, www.sweetyhigh.com/read/peyton-list-twins-interview-072616.

[xxvi] Oprah Magazine. (n.d.). *J.Lo Remembers "Laughing Hysterically" When She Found Out She Was Having Twins*. [online] Available at: https://www.oprahmag.com/life/relationships-love/a27307398/jennifer-lopez-pregnant-twins-emme-max-reaction-you-tube/ [Accessed 14 Dec. 2019].

[xxvii] Rydhström, H, and I Ingemarsson. "Interval between Birth of the First and the Second Twin and Its Impact on Second Twin Perinatal Mortality." *Journal of Perinatal Medicine*, U.S. National Library of Medicine, 1990, www.ncbi.nlm.nih.gov/pubmed/2097336.

[xxviii] Wilson, Julee. "Tia Mowry Is Our New Favorite Style Star. Here's Why..." *HuffPost*, HuffPost, 27 Jan. 2015, www.huffpost.com/entry/tia-mowry-style-star_n_6528960.

Printed in Great Britain
by Amazon